Brain-Boosting Bites & Guide: Alzheimer's & Dementia – A 2-in-1 Recipe & Care Manual for Families and Caregivers

Navigating Memory Care with Nutritious Cookbook and Proactive Strategies – The Complete Roadmap for Enhancing Cognitive Health

Richard Isaacs

Table of the Contents:

Defining Aging and Its Impact on Cognitive Function

As we embark on this journey together, it's essential first to understand the basics. What is aging, and how does it impact cognitive function? In this chapter, we'll explore these questions, drawing from the latest scientific research and expert consensus.

Section 1: What is Aging?

Aging is a natural biological process characterized by a gradual decline in the body's physical and physiological functions over time. It is a complex interplay of genetics, lifestyle, and environmental factors that influences every part of our being—from our skin's elasticity to our brain's cognitive abilities.

It's important to note that aging is not a disease but a fact of life. Everyone ages differently, and the rate of aging can be influenced by numerous factors. Factors like genetics, diet, physical activity, stress management, and environmental exposure can either speed up or slow down the aging process.

Section 2: Aging and the Brain

The brain, like any other organ in our body, is susceptible to the aging process. As we age, the brain undergoes several changes which can impact cognitive function. These changes include a decrease in volume, reduced blood flow, and a decline in the number and function of neurons, the nerve cells responsible for transmitting information in the brain.

However, these changes do not necessarily equate to cognitive decline. Cognitive aging, the changes in cognitive function that occur with age, is a normal part of aging and does not always lead to cognitive impairment or dementia.

Section 3: Cognitive Aging and Its Impact

Cognitive aging can manifest as subtle changes in several cognitive abilities, such as:

- Memory: Aging may affect episodic memory (remembering specific events) and working memory (briefly holding and manipulating information), while semantic memory (knowledge of facts and concepts) and procedural memory (how to perform tasks) remain relatively preserved.
- Attention: The ability to maintain focus may become slightly impaired with age, especially in situations that require divided attention.
- Processing Speed: The speed at which we process information tends to slow down as we age.
- Executive Function: These are complex cognitive processes that include planning, problem-solving, decision-making, and multi-tasking. Some aspects of executive function may become more challenging with age.

Section 4: The Spectrum of Cognitive Aging

It's crucial to realize that cognitive aging is not uniform. Just as people age physically at different rates and in different ways, so too does cognitive function vary significantly among individuals. Some people may experience noticeable changes in their cognitive abilities as they age, while others may not.

Cognitive Reserve is a concept used to explain this variance in cognitive aging. It refers to the brain's ability to improvise and find alternative ways of getting a job done. The cognitive reserve theory suggests that individuals with more robust cognitive reserves (often built through lifelong education, regular mental stimulation, physical activity, and social engagement) are better equipped to withstand the negative effects of aging and brain damage.

Section 5: Differentiating Between Normal Aging and Dementia

As noted, minor cognitive changes are a normal part of aging. However, when cognitive decline becomes severe enough to disrupt daily life, it could indicate a condition like dementia or Alzheimer's disease.

Dementia is a general term for a decline in mental ability severe enough to interfere with daily life. Alzheimer's disease is the most common type of dementia, accounting for 60-80% of cases. Other types of dementia include Vascular dementia, Lewy body dementia, and Frontotemporal dementia.

Unlike normal cognitive aging, dementia is characterized by significant memory loss, confusion, difficulty communicating, and mood changes. It is progressive, meaning it worsens over time, and it significantly impacts a person's ability to perform everyday activities.

Section 6: Promoting Cognitive Health

Understanding the distinction between normal cognitive aging and dementia is important, but equally essential is recognizing that there are steps we can take to promote cognitive health as we age:

- Regular Exercise: Physical activity increases blood flow to the whole body, including the brain, and can help enhance cognitive function.
- Balanced Diet: Consuming a diet rich in fruits, vegetables, lean protein, and healthy fats can help protect the brain.
- Mental Stimulation: Engaging in mentally stimulating activities, like puzzles, reading, or learning a new skill, can help build cognitive reserve.
- Social Engagement: Maintaining strong social networks can help stave off cognitive decline.

- Regular Check-ups: Regular medical check-ups can help identify potential health problems before they become severe and impact cognitive health.

Section 7: The Role of Genetics in Cognitive Aging

- While lifestyle plays a crucial role in cognitive aging, genetics also has a part to play. Certain genetic factors can make individuals more susceptible to significant cognitive decline, including the development of conditions such as Alzheimer's disease. For instance, the presence of the APOE-e4 allele is known to increase the risk. However, having a genetic predisposition does not guarantee that an individual will develop dementia or Alzheimer's, nor does the absence of such genes ensure protection. It's the interplay of genes, lifestyle, and environment that ultimately determines cognitive aging and the risk of dementia.

Section 8: The Impact of Stress on Cognitive Function

- Chronic stress can have a negative impact on cognitive function, particularly on areas of the brain vital for memory. It increases the production of the hormone cortisol, which in high amounts can impair memory. Effective stress management techniques, such as mindfulness, meditation, and regular exercise, can help maintain cognitive function as we age.

Section 9: Sleep and Cognitive Health

- Quality sleep is essential for cognitive function. While we sleep, our brains perform essential tasks such as consolidating memories and clearing out waste products. Chronic sleep deprivation or disruption can have detrimental effects on these processes and accelerate cognitive aging. Implementing good sleep hygiene practices is crucial for maintaining cognitive health.

Section 10: Mental Health and Cognitive Aging

- Mental health conditions such as depression and anxiety can have a substantial impact on cognitive function. Depression in later life can sometimes be mistaken for or precede the onset of dementia. Ensuring that mental health is well managed and treated is an essential aspect of cognitive care in older age.
- In the coming chapters, we will further delve into the signs and symptoms of cognitive disorders like dementia and Alzheimer's, different diagnostic methods, and treatment options currently available. We will also explore strategies to slow cognitive decline, offering practical tips on diet, exercise, and maintaining an active and engaging lifestyle. We will also address the often overlooked but critically important aspect of emotional well-being and support for those living with cognitive changes and their caregivers. By understanding aging and its impact on cognitive function, we can pave the way for a more empowered and hopeful approach to this natural phase of life.

Section 11: The Aging Brain and Neuroplasticity

- One of the most significant discoveries in neuroscience in recent decades is the concept of neuroplasticity - the brain's ability to reorganize itself and form new neural connections throughout life. This capacity does not disappear with age; it may diminish but it is never lost. Neuroplasticity can help counter the effects of aging and injury on the brain and is the basis for rehabilitation from brain damage. Engaging in novel, complex activities, especially those that require mental and physical engagement, can stimulate neuroplasticity and contribute to cognitive resilience even in older age.

Section 12: Cognitive Screening and Regular Check-ups

- Regular cognitive screenings can help detect cognitive impairment at an early stage, which allows for more timely intervention and potentially better outcomes. Screening methods range from brief questionnaires to more detailed neuropsychological tests that assess various aspects of cognition. These screenings, combined with routine physical check-ups, can help monitor cognitive health as one ages and can serve as a starting point for conversations about brain health with healthcare providers.

Section 13: Aging, Cognition, and Multilingualism

- Emerging research suggests that being multilingual can be beneficial for cognitive health. It can delay the onset of dementia symptoms by a few years, a phenomenon attributed to the enhanced cognitive reserve in multilingual individuals. Learning a new language at any age is a rewarding way to stimulate the brain, highlighting the brain's capacity to learn and adapt, irrespective of age.

Section 14: The Role of Social Connections in Cognitive Aging

- Social isolation and loneliness can have detrimental effects on cognitive health. On the other hand, maintaining strong social connections, engaging in group activities, and staying socially active can provide mental stimulation, emotional support, and contribute to a better quality of life, thus slowing cognitive decline.
- Section 15: Embracing Aging and Cognitive Changes
- Aging and the accompanying cognitive changes can be embraced as a natural part of life's journey. While it may bring challenges, it also brings wisdom, perspective, and can open new avenues for growth and learning. A proactive, informed approach to cognitive health can lead to healthier, more resilient aging. Cultivating a positive attitude towards aging, focusing on capability rather than loss, and continuing to set and pursue goals can contribute to overall well-being and life satisfaction in older age.

Differentiating Between Normal Memory Loss and Symptoms of Dementia

As we delve deeper into understanding cognitive function, it's crucial to distinguish between normal memory loss that comes with age and the more severe symptoms of dementia. Knowing the difference between these two will help identify when it's simply a part of the natural aging process or when it's time to seek professional help.

Section 1: Normal Age-Related Memory Loss

Normal age-related memory loss, often called "age-associated memory impairment," is a part of the natural aging process. We all forget things occasionally at all ages, but it tends to become more frequent as we get older. This type of memory loss is usually predictable and manageable. For example, you might forget the name of an acquaintance, misplace everyday items like glasses or keys, or struggle to recall a word on the tip of your tongue.

Crucially, while these moments might be frustrating, they don't generally disrupt our ability to live independently. We are still able to maintain a conversation, remember important life events, and manage daily tasks such as paying bills, cooking, or driving.

Section 2: Memory Loss in Dementia

Dementia, on the other hand, is marked by a consistent decline in memory and other cognitive functions that significantly impact daily life. Symptoms of dementia might include:

- Difficulty recalling recent events while often remembering distant past events clearly
- Frequently forgetting important dates, events, or personal history
- Repeating the same questions or stories within a short period

- Getting lost in familiar places
- Difficulty following directions
- Struggling to make decisions or solve problems that were once easy
- Inability to keep track of bills, appointments, or medications
- Changes in mood, personality, or behavior

The memory loss in dementia is more than just forgetfulness; it is a severe disruption to memory that hinders a person's ability to function independently.

Section 3: When to Seek Help

It's essential to note that everyone has forgetful moments, regardless of age. However, if memory problems become persistent and interfere with daily life, it's crucial to seek medical advice. It's particularly important if memory loss is accompanied by other cognitive symptoms like confusion, disorientation, language problems, or significant changes in personality or behavior.

Early detection of dementia provides the best chance of managing the disease effectively, delaying progression, and improving quality of life. There are many different causes of dementia, some of which are treatable, so it's essential to get a proper diagnosis.

Section 4: The Importance of a Comprehensive Assessment

Differentiating between normal memory loss and symptoms of dementia requires a comprehensive assessment by a healthcare professional. This assessment may include medical history, physical examination, laboratory tests, and cognitive tests that assess memory, thinking skills, problem-solving, attention, and language.

Overview of Alzheimer's Disease and Other Forms of Dementia

In our exploration of cognitive function and aging, it's essential to understand Alzheimer's disease and other forms of dementia, which represent more serious cognitive decline. In this chapter, we'll provide an overview of these conditions, their symptoms, progression, and current understandings of their causes.

Section 1: Understanding Dementia

Dementia is an umbrella term for a group of symptoms affecting memory, thinking abilities, and social skills severely enough to interfere with daily life. It is not a single disease but a term that encapsulates several conditions, each with its own causes and symptomatology. Dementia is a progressive condition, meaning the symptoms will gradually worsen over time.

Section 2: Alzheimer's Disease

Alzheimer's disease is the most common type of dementia, accounting for 60-80% of cases. It is characterized by the buildup of two types of protein in the brain: plaques (beta-amyloid) and tangles (tau). These proteins disrupt the communication between nerve cells and eventually lead to cell death.

Symptoms of Alzheimer's disease usually develop slowly and progress over time, becoming severe enough to interfere with daily tasks. It typically begins with mild memory loss, confusion, and difficulty completing familiar tasks. As the disease progresses, individuals may experience mood changes, increased confusion, difficulty speaking, swallowing, and walking.

Section 3: Vascular Dementia

Vascular dementia, the second most common type of dementia, is often caused by conditions that block or reduce blood flow to the brain, depriving brain cells of essential oxygen and nutrients. Symptoms can vary depending on the areas of the brain affected and may include problems with short-term memory, organizing thoughts, or managing money.

Section 4: Lewy Body Dementia

Lewy body dementia is characterized by the buildup of Lewy bodies (protein deposits) in the brain. This form of dementia shares characteristics with both Alzheimer's and Parkinson's diseases. Symptoms may include visual hallucinations, issues with attention and alertness, and Parkinsonian symptoms such as a shuffling walk and tremors.

Section 5: Frontotemporal Dementia

Frontotemporal dementia refers to a group of disorders caused by progressive nerve cell loss in the frontal and temporal lobes of the brain. These areas of the brain are associated with personality, behavior, and language. Symptoms may include personality and behavior changes, difficulty with language and speech, and problems with movement.

Section 6: Mixed Dementia

Mixed dementia is a condition in which a person has more than one type of dementia. For instance, a person could have both Alzheimer's disease and vascular dementia simultaneously. The symptoms often reflect the symptoms of the different types involved.

Early Detection and Diagnosis

Understanding the early signs of memory loss and dementia, along with the importance of early diagnosis, is crucial in managing these conditions effectively. This chapter will guide you through the initial signs of cognitive impairment, highlight the value of early diagnosis, and discuss the various medical examinations and tests used to diagnose dementia.

Section 1: Recognizing the Early Signs of Memory Loss and Dementia

Early signs of memory loss and dementia often involve subtle changes in cognitive function and behavior. These signs may include:

- Frequent forgetfulness, especially of recent events or conversations
- Difficulty performing familiar tasks
- Confusion about time and place
- Difficulty with words and conversation
- Changes in mood, personality, or behavior
- Difficulty with problem-solving or planning

While some level of forgetfulness can be a normal part of aging, consistent or increasing difficulties with memory, cognition, or behavior may warrant further investigation.

Section 2: The Importance of Early Diagnosis

The early diagnosis of dementia provides several benefits:

- It allows individuals and families to plan for the future, make living arrangements, settle financial matters, and establish care preferences.

- It provides more time to manage comorbid conditions, adjust medications, and focus on overall health and wellness, which can slow the progression of dementia.
- It allows for early interventions, which can enhance quality of life, manage symptoms, and prolong independence.
- It provides the opportunity to participate in clinical trials for new treatments.

Section 3: Medical Examinations and Tests for Diagnosing Dementia

The diagnostic process for dementia involves a series of steps to rule out other possible causes of symptoms. Here's what the process generally looks like:

- Medical History: A thorough review of medical history, including an evaluation of symptoms, duration, and family history of cognitive disorders.
- Physical Examination: A general physical exam to check for health issues that could affect cognitive function.
- Neurological Examination: Checks for signs of stroke, Parkinson's disease, tumors, or other medical conditions that can impair brain function.
- Cognitive and Neuropsychological Tests: These tests assess memory, problem-solving, attention, counting, and language skills.
- Brain Imaging: Techniques such as MRI or CT scans can detect brain abnormalities or changes linked to dementia.
- Laboratory Tests: Blood tests can help rule out non-dementia causes of memory impairment, like vitamin B-12 deficiency or an underactive thyroid gland.

A diagnosis of dementia often requires a careful medical evaluation by a specialist, such as a neurologist, psychiatrist, or geriatrician. The process can take time and patience.

Early detection and diagnosis of dementia are critical for optimal management of the disease. Understanding the signs and the diagnostic process can empower individuals and families to seek help promptly, offering the best opportunity to live a full, vibrant life, even after a dementia diagnosis.

Medical Treatment Options

The journey with dementia and Alzheimer's disease is undeniably challenging, but numerous medical treatments can help manage symptoms, improve quality of life, and slow disease progression. This chapter will outline the current options for medication management, highlight the latest research and advancements in treatment, and discuss potential side effects and their management.

Section 1: Medication Management for Dementia and Alzheimer's Disease

Currently, there is no cure for Alzheimer's disease and most other forms of dementia. However, several medications have been developed that can help manage the symptoms. These include:

- Cholinesterase inhibitors: These drugs, including donepezil, rivastigmine, and galantamine, work by boosting levels of a chemical messenger involved in memory and judgment. They can help alleviate symptoms for a time in some individuals with Alzheimer's.
- Memantine: This medication works by regulating the activity of glutamate, a chemical messenger involved in brain functions such as learning and memory. Memantine can delay progression of symptoms in moderate to severe Alzheimer's for some people.
- Combined drugs: A combination of memantine and a cholinesterase inhibitor can be more beneficial for some people.

Additionally, medications to manage other symptoms or related conditions, such as sleep disturbances, depression, anxiety, and agitation, may be prescribed.

Section 2: The Latest Research and Advancements in Treatment

Research into Alzheimer's disease and other forms of dementia is vibrant and ongoing. New drugs and treatment strategies are continually being explored. Recent developments include:

- Anti-amyloid beta therapies: These are designed to reduce the accumulation of amyloid beta proteins in the brain, which form the plaques associated with Alzheimer's disease.
- Tau protein inhibitors: These aim to inhibit the tau protein, which forms tangles in the brains of people with Alzheimer's.
- Neuroprotective drugs: These are designed to protect neurons from the damage caused by Alzheimer's, thereby slowing or preventing disease progression.

Many of these potential treatments are still in experimental stages or clinical trials, but they represent promising directions in Alzheimer's and dementia treatment research.

Section 3: Potential Side Effects and How to Manage Them

Like all medications, those used to treat dementia and Alzheimer's disease can have side effects. These may include nausea, vomiting, appetite loss, and increased frequency of bowel movements with cholinesterase inhibitors, or dizziness, headache, confusion, and constipation with memantine.

Management of these side effects often involves adjusting the dose, changing the medication, or providing additional treatments to manage the side effects. It's essential for individuals and their caregivers to communicate any side effects to their healthcare provider to ensure optimal treatment.

Nutrition and Physical Health

Physical health, including diet and exercise, plays a critical role in maintaining cognitive function and can significantly influence the course of dementia and memory loss. This chapter will discuss the impact of diet on cognitive function, provide nutritional advice for those with dementia or memory loss, and underline the importance of physical activity and exercise.

Section 1: Role of Diet in Cognitive Function

Diet has a direct impact on brain health. Certain nutrients and eating patterns can support brain health, slow the progression of dementia, and improve memory and mood. The Mediterranean diet, high in fruits, vegetables, whole grains, olive oil, and lean protein, is often associated with lower rates of dementia. Other beneficial dietary components include:

- Omega-3 fatty acids, found in fatty fish and flaxseeds, which can slow cognitive decline.
- Antioxidants, found in berries, dark chocolate, nuts, and vegetables, which can protect the brain from damage.
- Vitamins E and B, found in nuts, seeds, leafy greens, and whole grains, which can support brain health and slow the progression of Alzheimer's disease.

Section 2: Nutritional Advice for Those with Dementia or Memory Loss

For individuals with dementia or memory loss, maintaining a healthy diet can be challenging, but essential. Here are some nutritional strategies:

- Encourage regular, balanced meals filled with a variety of fruits, vegetables, lean proteins, and whole grains.
- Ensure adequate hydration, as seniors are more susceptible to dehydration.
- Use spices and herbs to enhance taste if medications affect the sense of taste.
- Provide healthy snacks to ensure sufficient caloric intake if meal sizes become smaller.
- Consider professional dietary advice if weight loss, swallowing difficulties, or a lack of appetite become serious concerns.

Section 3: Importance of Physical Activity and Exercise

Regular physical activity and exercise are crucial in managing dementia and memory loss. Exercise can improve heart health, increase energy levels, improve mood and sleep, and reduce the risk of chronic diseases. It can also improve brain health by increasing blood flow and promoting growth and survival of neurons.

Exercise routines should be safe, enjoyable, and match the individual's abilities. Walking, swimming, dancing, or gentle yoga are all good options. Incorporating physical activity into daily routines, such as walking during errands, can also be beneficial.

The Power of Routine and Familiar Environment

One of the less recognized but highly effective ways to manage dementia symptoms is through maintaining regular routines and creating a dementia-friendly environment. This chapter will guide you through building daily routines to provide consistency and memory aid, as well as designing an environment conducive to the needs of someone with dementia.

Section 1: Building Daily Routines for Consistency and Memory Aid

Establishing and maintaining daily routines can significantly benefit those with dementia. Routine provides structure, reduces confusion, and can enhance feelings of safety and comfort. It can also reduce agitation and improve sleep. When creating a routine:

- Incorporate activities the person enjoys and can perform with a degree of independence. These can range from personal care tasks to hobbies or exercise.
- Make sure to keep meal times and bedtimes consistent.
- Allow plenty of time for each activity, reducing the need to rush, which can cause confusion or stress.
- Be flexible. If a particular part of the routine causes distress, it's okay to change it.

Section 2: Designing a Dementia-Friendly Environment

The environment can significantly impact a person with dementia's ability to function and their overall wellbeing. A dementia-friendly environment minimizes confusion, enhances safety, and promotes independence. Here are some things to consider:

- Safety: Install locks on doors and windows, use safety devices on stoves and ovens, remove tripping hazards, and ensure the home is well-lit to prevent falls.
- Simplify: Avoid clutter and keep the environment as straightforward as possible. Too many choices or stimuli can be overwhelming.
- Familiarity: Surround the person with familiar objects and photos to provide a sense of comfort and aid memory.
- Signage: Label rooms and cupboards with words or pictures to help the person navigate their environment.

By leveraging the power of routine and a familiar environment, you can provide additional support for a loved one with dementia.

Legal and Financial Planning

Dealing with dementia involves more than medical treatments and care strategies; it also requires forward-thinking legal and financial planning. This chapter will underscore the importance of early legal and financial planning, guide you through matters such as power of attorney, wills, and other legal issues, and help you understand insurance and long-term care options.

Section 1: Importance of Early Legal and Financial Planning

The earlier legal and financial planning begins, the more the person with dementia may be able to participate in decision-making. Early planning allows for more time to explore options, make sense of legal and financial matters, and ensure the person's wishes are understood and respected. Key elements of planning include understanding the cost of care, organizing important documents, making plans for finances and property, and identifying potential care options.

Section 2: Guiding Through Power of Attorney, Wills, and Other Legal Issues

Legal planning for dementia involves considering several types of legal documents:

- Power of Attorney: A power of attorney for finances and healthcare allows the person with dementia to appoint another individual to make decisions on their behalf when they are no longer able.
- Will: This legal document outlines how the person's assets and estate will be distributed upon their death.
- Living Will: This outlines the person's wishes for end-of-life medical care.

Legal counsel should be sought to ensure all these documents are correctly drawn up and adhere to all legal requirements in your jurisdiction.

Section 3: Understanding Insurance and Long-Term Care Options

Understanding the different types of care and how to finance them is critical. Options can vary greatly in cost, and different insurance plans cover different types of care:

- Health Insurance: These policies may cover certain medical costs associated with dementia, such as doctor visits and medication, but they typically do not cover long-term care.
- Long-Term Care Insurance: These policies can help cover the cost of long-term care services, such as home care, assisted living, or nursing home care.
- Medicare/Medicaid: These programs may cover some costs associated with dementia, but eligibility and coverage can be complex. It's important to thoroughly research and understand what these programs cover.

Financial and legal planning for dementia can be complex, but they are crucial elements of the care journey. Consulting with legal and financial professionals can help ensure a solid plan is in place.

Benefits of the Mind Diet

Our brains, those intricate powerhouses that run the show, need the right fuel to function at their best. The MIND (Mediterranean-DASH Diet Intervention for Neurodegenerative Delay) diet, a marriage between the heart-healthy Mediterranean diet and the blood pressure-lowering DASH (Dietary Approaches to Stop Hypertension) diet, has been specially designed to lower the risk of Alzheimer's and improve cognitive health.

The MIND diet is rich in nutrient-dense foods that boost brain health, like berries, leafy greens, nuts, fish, and olive oil. It also limits consumption of foods that may harm the brain over time, such as red meat, cheese, sweets, and fried or fast food.

So, what are the benefits of following the MIND diet? Here are a few key ones:

1. Enhanced Cognitive Function: The MIND diet can enhance memory and cognitive abilities. Foods rich in antioxidants like berries and leafy greens can fight off free radicals, thereby reducing oxidative stress, which is known to contribute to brain aging and cognitive decline.

2. Reduced Risk of Alzheimer's and Dementia: Studies have shown that people who adhere closely to the MIND diet have a significantly lower risk of developing Alzheimer's disease and other forms of dementia.

3. Improved Heart Health: The MIND diet includes foods that are good for the heart, such as fish, nuts, and whole grains. These foods can help lower blood pressure and bad cholesterol, reducing the risk of heart disease.

4. Weight Management: High in fiber and low in unhealthy fats, the MIND diet can help you maintain a healthy weight, which is beneficial not only for overall health but also for the brain, as obesity is a risk factor for cognitive decline.

5. Mood Enhancement: A diet rich in vitamins, minerals, and other nutrients can contribute to better mental health. Foods like fruits, vegetables, and whole grains can improve mood and reduce the risk of depression.

Incorporating the MIND diet into your lifestyle could be one of the most powerful moves you make for your brain health. As you explore "The Ultimate Mind/Brain Diet Recipes For Seniors", each recipe will carry with it the benefits of this diet, bringing a fusion of flavor and health to your table. So, let's begin this journey towards nourishing your brain and delighting your palate!

Mental Exercises and Cognitive Therapy

Alongside physical health, mental exercises and cognitive therapies can play a significant role in managing dementia and memory loss. This chapter will discuss mental exercises designed to improve memory and cognition, explore the role of cognitive behavioral therapy, and examine how technology can be used for mental stimulation.

Section 1: Mental Exercises to Improve Memory and Cognition

Mental or cognitive exercises are tasks designed to stimulate thinking skills, memory, and cognitive abilities. They often involve activities that require memory, reasoning, attention, and flexibility of thinking. Examples include:

- Puzzle solving: Crosswords, Sudoku, and jigsaw puzzles can help engage the brain's problem-solving faculties.

- Memory exercises: Activities such as memorizing a poem, learning a new language, or playing a memory card game can stimulate the memory function.
- Artistic activities: Painting, playing an instrument, or learning to dance can engage multiple areas of the brain.

Section 2: Role of Cognitive Behavioral Therapy

Cognitive Behavioral Therapy (CBT) can be beneficial for individuals with dementia, especially those dealing with anxiety, depression, or agitation. CBT works by helping individuals identify and change patterns of thought that lead to negative behaviors or emotions. While CBT does not slow the progression of dementia, it can significantly improve the quality of life and ease the burden of caregivers by addressing behavioral symptoms.

Section 3: Using Technology for Mental Stimulation

Technology can offer unique and engaging ways of providing mental stimulation:

- Brain-training apps: These apps offer a range of activities designed to improve various cognitive skills such as memory, attention, and problem-solving.
- Virtual reality: Immersive experiences can provide mental stimulation and even allow for virtual travel, which can be particularly beneficial for those unable to leave their homes.
- Audiobooks and e-books: These can make reading accessible even to those with visual impairment or physical difficulties in handling a book.

In conclusion, mental exercises and cognitive therapy offer effective methods of managing dementia symptoms and improving cognitive health. These methods can be used in conjunction with medical treatments and physical health strategies to provide a holistic approach to dementia care.

Emotional Support and Coping Mechanisms

The journey with dementia is not only about memory loss but also involves considerable emotional and psychological impacts. Providing emotional support and fostering coping mechanisms are essential aspects of dementia care. This chapter will discuss the emotional and psychological impact of memory loss, suggest ways to support the emotional needs of individuals with dementia, and explore strategies for stress management and relaxation.

Section 1: Dealing with the Emotional and Psychological Impact of Memory Loss

Memory loss and cognitive decline can lead to a range of emotional reactions, including confusion, frustration, anxiety, depression, and fear. It's essential to understand these reactions and empathize with the emotional toll they take on the individual. Encourage open communication about these feelings and reassure them that it's okay to feel upset or worried. Mental health professionals, like psychologists or therapists, can also provide necessary emotional support and strategies to cope with these emotions.

Section 2: Supporting the Emotional Needs of Individuals with Dementia

People with dementia often experience feelings of loss, fear, and disorientation. Providing emotional support can help alleviate these feelings:

- Maintain dignity and respect: Regardless of cognitive impairment, treat the individual with dignity, kindness, and respect.
- Provide reassurance: Frequent reassurance can help reduce anxiety and provide comfort.

- Encourage social interaction: Encourage them to participate in family gatherings, clubs, or social events as much as they feel comfortable.
- Focus on remaining abilities: Celebrate what they can do rather than mourning what they cannot. This can bolster self-esteem and feelings of worth.

Section 3: Strategies for Stress Management and Relaxation

Stress can exacerbate dementia symptoms. Implementing strategies for relaxation can help manage stress levels:

- Practice mindfulness: Techniques such as deep breathing, meditation, or gentle yoga can help reduce anxiety and promote relaxation.
- Encourage enjoyable activities: Hobbies or activities that the person enjoys can be therapeutic and provide a sense of normalcy.
- Promote regular exercise: Physical activity can reduce stress, improve mood, and promote better sleep.
- Consider professional support: Therapists specializing in cognitive behavioral therapy can provide coping strategies to manage stress effectively.

Caring for emotional health is as important as tending to physical and cognitive needs in dementia care. By recognizing and addressing the emotional impact of dementia, and by fostering stress management and relaxation strategies, we can significantly improve the quality of life for those living with dementia.

Community Resources and Support Systems

Living with dementia or caring for a loved one with dementia can often feel overwhelming, but you don't have to navigate this journey alone. Numerous community resources and support systems can provide help. This chapter will guide you in navigating resources available for dementia patients and their families, building a support network within your community, and choosing the right residential care option, if necessary.

Section 1: Navigating Resources Available for Dementia Patients and Their Families

Various organizations provide resources for dementia patients and their families, such as informational materials, support groups, counseling services, and more. Some of these resources include:

- Alzheimer's Association: Offers comprehensive information about Alzheimer's disease and dementia, support groups, a 24/7 helpline, educational programs, and advocacy resources.
- Area Agencies on Aging (AAA): Provides a wide range of services to seniors and their families, including care planning, in-home services, meals, transportation, and legal aid.
- Online forums and websites: Websites such as the Alzheimer's Reading Room, Alzheimer's Foundation of America, and various online communities offer a wealth of information and platforms for sharing experiences and advice.

Section 2: Building a Support Network within Your Community

Building a strong support network is crucial. This network can include family, friends, neighbors, volunteers, and community members. They can provide emotional support, respite care, assistance with errands, or simply companionship. Also, consider joining support groups for caregivers or families dealing with dementia. Sharing your experiences with people in similar situations can provide emotional relief and practical advice.

Section 3: How to Choose the Right Residential Care Option if Necessary

Sometimes, home care may not be a feasible option, and residential care may be necessary. When considering residential care, keep the following factors in mind:

- Level of care: Does the facility provide the necessary level of care for your loved one's current and future needs?
- Staff: Is the staff trained and experienced in dementia care? Is the staff-to-resident ratio adequate?
- Environment: Is the environment safe, comfortable, and conducive to the needs of a person with dementia?
- Activities: Does the facility offer activities that your loved one will enjoy and benefit from?
- Costs: Are the costs transparent and within your budget?

Choosing the right residential care is a significant decision and should involve the individual with dementia, as much as possible, as well as family members or trusted advisors.

In conclusion, navigating the journey of dementia can be challenging, but you are not alone. A wealth of community resources and support systems are available, and taking advantage of them can significantly improve the quality of life for both the person with dementia and their caregivers.

Caring for the Caregiver

While the focus of dementia care often centers on the individual with the disease, it's equally important to acknowledge the caregivers' role and the impact this journey has on them. This chapter will recognize the strain on caregivers and family members, provide strategies for managing caregiver stress, and share resources for caregiver support.

Section 1: Recognizing the Strain on Caregivers and Family Members

Caregiving for a loved one with dementia can be rewarding, but it also comes with significant emotional, physical, and sometimes financial strain. It's essential to recognize signs of caregiver stress and burnout, which might include feelings of overwhelm, social withdrawal, fatigue, health problems, and feelings of resentment or irritation.

Section 2: Strategies for Managing Caregiver Stress

Maintaining the caregiver's health and wellbeing is crucial for their ability to provide effective care. Here are some strategies to manage caregiver stress:

- Practice self-care: Regular exercise, a balanced diet, and sufficient sleep are foundational to physical health and stress management.
- Seek support: Join a caregiver support group where you can share experiences and coping strategies.
- Take breaks: Respite care provides temporary relief for caregivers. This can be a few hours of in-home care or short-term residential care.
- Practice mindfulness: Techniques such as meditation, deep breathing, or yoga can reduce stress and promote relaxation.
- Ask for help: Don't hesitate to ask family, friends, or community resources for help.

Section 3: Resources for Caregiver Support

Several resources offer support specifically for caregivers:

- Family Caregiver Alliance: Provides a wealth of information on caregiving, along with resources such as online support groups, webinars, and fact sheets.
- National Alliance for Caregiving: Offers free resources and information on caregiving, as well as advocacy for caregiver issues.
- Local services: Many communities offer local resources such as respite care services, adult daycare, meal delivery, and more.

In conclusion, caring for the caregiver is a crucial aspect of the dementia care journey. Caregivers should remember that their health and wellbeing matter and are key to their ability to care for their loved ones. While the journey through dementia can be difficult, remember that there are resources and support available. You don't have to navigate this journey alone.

Looking to the Future

The journey through dementia can often feel daunting, but it is important to look ahead with hope and positivity. This concluding chapter will discuss current research and what it means for the future of dementia treatment, the importance of living positively with dementia, and provide concluding thoughts and resources for further support.

Section 1: Current Research and What it Means for the Future of Dementia Treatment

Dementia research is a dynamic and evolving field. Scientists and researchers worldwide are working tirelessly to understand the complexities of the disease, develop effective treatments, and, ultimately, find a cure. Advances in technology and genomics are enabling more in-depth research into the causes of dementia and potential therapeutic targets. While we are not there yet, these research efforts bring hope that more effective treatments, and perhaps even a cure, may be on the horizon.

Section 2: Living Positively with Dementia

Despite the challenges dementia presents, it is possible to live well and positively with the condition. Focusing on the person rather than the disease, emphasizing abilities rather than deficits, maintaining a sense of humor, and celebrating small victories can significantly enhance quality of life. Creating a supportive and enabling environment, continuing to engage in enjoyable activities, and maintaining social interactions can help foster positivity and wellbeing.

Section 3: Concluding Thoughts and Resources for Further Support

In conclusion, dementia is a challenging journey, but it is one that no one has to walk alone. Resources and support are available, and it is important to remember to take care of oneself in addition to caring for a loved one with dementia.

Embrace the support of friends, family, and the wider community. Stay informed about the latest research and treatments. Celebrate the good moments, and don't forget to laugh. This journey may not be one you would have chosen, but it can be navigated with grace, strength, and resilience.

For further information and support, the Alzheimer's Association, Alzheimer's Foundation of America, and local community health and social services are invaluable resources. Remember that help is available, and it's okay to reach out when you need it.

Here's to a future where we better understand dementia, have more effective treatments, and perhaps, one day, a world without dementia. Until then, we navigate this path together, armed with knowledge, understanding, and empathy.

Recipes

Breakfast

Blueberry Almond Overnight Oats

Ingredients:

- 1/2 cup oats
- 1/2 cup almond milk
- 1/2 cup fresh blueberries
- 1 tablespoon chia seeds
- 1 tablespoon honey
- 1 tablespoon almond butter
- A handful of almond flakes for garnish

Steps:

1. In a jar, combine the oats, almond milk, and chia seeds.
2. Stir in the honey and almond butter until well mixed.
3. Top with fresh blueberries and almond flakes.
4. Cover and refrigerate overnight.
5. In the morning, give it a good stir and enjoy cold or warmed up.

Nutritional Values: Calories: 350 kcal, Protein: 10g, Fiber: 9g, Omega-3 fatty acids: 2g

---

Smoked Salmon Avocado Toast

Ingredients:

- 2 slices of whole grain bread

- 1 ripe avocado
- 4 slices of smoked salmon
- 1 tablespoon of lemon juice
- Salt and pepper to taste
- Fresh dill for garnish

Steps:

1. Toast the bread slices until golden brown.
2. In a bowl, mash the ripe avocado and add lemon juice, salt, and pepper.
3. Spread the mashed avocado evenly over the toasted bread slices.
4. Top each slice with two pieces of smoked salmon.
5. Garnish with fresh dill and serve.

Nutritional Values: Calories: 400 kcal, Protein: 20g, Fiber: 7g, Omega-3 fatty acids: 1.5g

---

Egg and Spinach Scramble

Ingredients:

- 2 large eggs
- 2 cups of fresh spinach
- 1 tablespoon of olive oil
- Salt and pepper to taste
- A sprinkle of grated parmesan

Steps:

1. Heat olive oil in a non-stick pan over medium heat.
2. Add spinach and cook until wilted.
3. Beat the eggs in a bowl and add to the pan, stirring occasionally.
4. Once the eggs are almost cooked, season with salt and pepper.
5. Sprinkle with grated parmesan and serve.

Nutritional Values: Calories: 300 kcal, Protein: 15g, Fiber: 2g, Omega-3 fatty acids: 0.4g

Each of these recipes is high in Omega-3 fatty acids and fiber, both of which are crucial for brain health and function. They are also lower in calories, helping maintain a healthy weight, and are easy to prepare, making them perfect for seniors.

Quinoa Fruit Salad

Ingredients:

- 1 cup cooked quinoa
- 1/2 cup blueberries
- 1/2 cup sliced strawberries
- 1/2 cup diced mango
- 1 tablespoon honey
- 1 tablespoon freshly squeezed lemon juice
- A sprinkle of chia seeds for garnish

Steps:

1. In a large bowl, combine cooked quinoa, blueberries, strawberries, and mango.
2. Drizzle honey and lemon juice over the fruit and quinoa.
3. Gently toss everything together until well combined.
4. Sprinkle with chia seeds and serve.

Nutritional Values: Calories: 300 kcal, Protein: 8g, Fiber: 7g, Omega-3 fatty acids: 0.5g

Nutty Banana Smoothie

Ingredients:

- 1 ripe banana
- 1 cup almond milk
- 1 tablespoon almond butter
- 1 tablespoon chia seeds
- A dash of cinnamon

Steps:

1. In a blender, combine the ripe banana, almond milk, almond butter, and chia seeds.
2. Blend until smooth and creamy.
3. Pour into a glass and sprinkle with a dash of cinnamon.
4. Serve immediately.

Nutritional Values: Calories: 250 kcal, Protein: 6g, Fiber: 7g, Omega-3 fatty acids: 2.5g

---

Greek Yogurt Parfait

Ingredients:

- 1 cup Greek yogurt
- 1 tablespoon honey
- 1/2 cup mixed berries (blueberries, strawberries, raspberries)
- 2 tablespoons granola
- A sprinkle of flaxseeds

Steps:

1. Layer half of the Greek yogurt in a glass or jar.
2. Top with half of the mixed berries and half of the granola.

3. Drizzle with half of the honey.
4. Repeat with the remaining yogurt, berries, granola, and honey.
5. Sprinkle with flaxseeds on top and serve.

Nutritional Values: Calories: 250 kcal, Protein: 20g, Fiber: 4g, Omega-3 fatty acids: 1.5g

These recipes are all easy to prepare, making them perfect for seniors. They are also high in nutrients known to promote brain health, such as omega-3 fatty acids and antioxidants. Enjoy these delicious breakfast options while nourishing your brain at the same time!

Green Smoothie Bowl

Ingredients:

- 1 ripe banana
- 1 cup of spinach or kale
- 1/2 cup almond milk
- 1 tablespoon chia seeds
- 1/2 cup of your favorite fruits (berries, mango, kiwi, etc.) for topping
- A sprinkle of coconut flakes for garnish

Steps:

1. In a blender, combine the ripe banana, spinach or kale, almond milk, and chia seeds.
2. Blend until smooth and creamy.
3. Pour into a bowl and top with your favorite fruits and a sprinkle of coconut flakes.
4. Serve immediately.

Nutritional Values: Calories: 280 kcal, Protein: 8g, Fiber: 8g, Omega-3 fatty acids: 2g

Almond and Date Porridge

Ingredients:

- 1/2 cup oats
- 1 cup almond milk
- 2 dates, pitted and chopped
- 1 tablespoon almond butter
- A sprinkle of cinnamon

Steps:

1. In a pot, combine oats, almond milk, and dates.
2. Bring to a boil, then reduce heat and simmer until oats are cooked and creamy.
3. Stir in almond butter and sprinkle with cinnamon.
4. Serve warm.

Nutritional Values: Calories: 350 kcal, Protein: 10g, Fiber: 7g, Omega-3 fatty acids: 2g

Scrambled Tofu with Veggies

Ingredients:

- 1 cup firm tofu, crumbled
- 1 tablespoon olive oil
- 1/2 cup bell peppers, diced
- 1/2 cup mushrooms, sliced
- Salt and pepper to taste
- A sprinkle of turmeric and paprika

Steps:

1. Heat olive oil in a non-stick pan over medium heat.
2. Add bell peppers and mushrooms, cook until tender.
3. Add crumbled tofu to the pan, stirring occasionally.
4. Season with salt, pepper, turmeric, and paprika.
5. Cook for a few more minutes, then serve.

Nutritional Values: Calories: 250 kcal, Protein: 20g, Fiber: 5g, Omega-3 fatty acids: 0.5g

Each of these recipes is high in protein, fiber, and omega-3 fatty acids, providing your brain with the nutrients it needs to stay healthy. Plus, they are easy to prepare and full of delicious flavors, perfect for seniors looking to maintain a healthy lifestyle.

Spinach and Feta Frittata

Ingredients:

- 4 large eggs
- 2 cups fresh spinach
- 1/2 cup feta cheese, crumbled
- 1 tablespoon olive oil
- Salt and pepper to taste

Steps:

1. Preheat the oven to 350°F (175°C).
2. In a bowl, beat the eggs and season with salt and pepper.
3. Heat olive oil in an oven-safe skillet over medium heat.
4. Add spinach and cook until wilted.
5. Pour the eggs over the spinach and sprinkle with crumbled feta.
6. Transfer the skillet to the oven and bake for 10-15 minutes until the eggs are set.
7. Let cool for a few minutes before serving.

Nutritional Values: Calories: 300 kcal, Protein: 20g, Fiber: 1g, Omega-3 fatty acids: 0.3g

---

Berry Nutty Quinoa

Ingredients:

- 1 cup cooked quinoa
- 1/2 cup mixed berries (strawberries, blueberries, raspberries)
- 2 tablespoons chopped nuts (almonds, walnuts, pecans)
- 1 tablespoon honey
- A sprinkle of chia seeds

Steps:

1. In a bowl, combine cooked quinoa, mixed berries, and chopped nuts.
2. Drizzle with honey and sprinkle with chia seeds.
3. Serve immediately.

Nutritional Values: Calories: 320 kcal, Protein: 10g, Fiber: 6g, Omega-3 fatty acids: 1.5g

---

Avocado and Tomato on Rye

Ingredients:

- 2 slices of rye bread
- 1 ripe avocado
- 1 tomato, sliced
- Salt and pepper to taste
- A drizzle of olive oil

Steps:

1. Toast the rye bread slices until golden brown.
2. Spread the ripe avocado evenly over the toasted slices.
3. Top with tomato slices, then season with salt and pepper.
4. Drizzle with a little olive oil and serve.

Nutritional Values: Calories: 300 kcal, Protein: 8g, Fiber: 10g, Omega-3 fatty acids: 0.5g

Each of these breakfast options is designed to provide seniors with the essential nutrients required for brain health. They are all high in Omega-3 fatty acids and fiber, low in unhealthy fats, and relatively low in calories. Plus, they are straightforward to prepare, making them ideal for seniors.

Chia Pudding with Fresh Berries

Ingredients:

- 1/4 cup chia seeds
- 1 cup almond milk
- 1 tablespoon honey
- 1/2 cup mixed berries (strawberries, blueberries, raspberries)

Steps:

1. In a jar, combine the chia seeds and almond milk.
2. Stir in the honey until well mixed.
3. Cover and refrigerate overnight.
4. In the morning, top with fresh berries and serve.

Nutritional Values: Calories: 300 kcal, Protein: 8g, Fiber: 12g, Omega-3 fatty acids: 4g

Veggie Omelette

Ingredients:

- 3 large eggs
- 1/2 cup mixed vegetables (bell peppers, tomatoes, spinach, mushrooms)
- 1 tablespoon olive oil
- Salt and pepper to taste

Steps:

1. In a bowl, beat the eggs and season with salt and pepper.
2. Heat olive oil in a non-stick pan over medium heat.
3. Add mixed vegetables and cook until tender.
4. Pour the eggs over the vegetables, let cook until the bottom is set.
5. Carefully flip the omelette and cook the other side.
6. Once done, slide onto a plate and serve.

Nutritional Values: Calories: 300 kcal, Protein: 18g, Fiber: 3g, Omega-3 fatty acids: 0.4g

Apple Cinnamon Porridge

Ingredients:

- 1/2 cup oats
- 1 cup almond milk
- 1 apple, diced
- 1 teaspoon cinnamon
- 1 tablespoon honey

Steps:

1. In a pot, combine oats, almond milk, and diced apple.
2. Bring to a boil, then reduce heat and simmer until oats are cooked and creamy.
3. Stir in cinnamon and honey.
4. Serve warm.

Nutritional Values: Calories: 350 kcal, Protein: 8g, Fiber: 7g, Omega-3 fatty acids: 2g

These breakfast recipes are designed to be nutritious, delicious, and senior-friendly. Each recipe provides a healthy dose of brain-boosting nutrients like Omega-3 fatty acids, fiber, and antioxidants. The ingredients used are not only good for your brain but also your overall health.

Baked Berries with Oat Topping

Ingredients:

- 2 cups mixed berries (raspberries, blackberries, blueberries)
- 1 cup oats
- 1/4 cup almond flour
- 1/4 cup honey
- 2 tablespoons coconut oil
- A dash of cinnamon

Steps:

1. Preheat your oven to 350°F (175°C).
2. In a baking dish, spread out the mixed berries.
3. In a separate bowl, combine oats, almond flour, honey, coconut oil, and cinnamon.
4. Sprinkle this mixture over the berries.

5. Bake for 25-30 minutes, until the topping is golden and the berries are bubbling.
6. Allow to cool slightly before serving.

Nutritional Values: Calories: 250 kcal, Protein: 5g, Fiber: 5g, Omega-3 fatty acids: 0.2g

---

Power Green Smoothie

Ingredients:

- 1 cup spinach or kale
- 1 banana
- 1/2 cup blueberries
- 1 tablespoon chia seeds
- 1 cup almond milk

Steps:

1. In a blender, combine spinach or kale, banana, blueberries, chia seeds, and almond milk.
2. Blend until smooth and creamy.
3. Pour into a glass and serve immediately.

Nutritional Values: Calories: 220 kcal, Protein: 6g, Fiber: 8g, Omega-3 fatty acids: 2g

---

Veggie Scramble with Whole Grain Toast

Ingredients:

- 2 large eggs
- 1 cup mixed veggies (bell peppers, spinach, mushrooms)

- 1 tablespoon olive oil
- 2 slices of whole grain bread
- Salt and pepper to taste

Steps:

1. Heat olive oil in a non-stick pan over medium heat.
2. Add the veggies and sauté until tender.
3. Beat the eggs in a bowl and add them to the pan, stirring occasionally.
4. Toast the bread while the eggs are cooking.
5. Season the scrambled eggs with salt and pepper.
6. Serve the eggs with the toasted bread.

Nutritional Values: Calories: 350 kcal, Protein: 16g, Fiber: 6g, Omega-3 fatty acids: 0.3g

These brain-boosting breakfast recipes provide a variety of options that are easy to prepare and full of the nutrients that seniors need. Each recipe includes a balance of protein, fiber, and omega-3 fatty acids, promoting overall health and cognitive function.

Buckwheat Pancakes with Blueberries

Ingredients:

- 1 cup buckwheat flour
- 1 cup almond milk
- 1 egg
- 1 tablespoon honey
- 1/2 cup fresh blueberries
- Coconut oil for cooking

Steps:

1. In a bowl, combine the buckwheat flour, almond milk, egg, and honey. Stir until well mixed.
2. Heat a small amount of coconut oil in a non-stick pan over medium heat.
3. Pour 1/4 cup of batter into the pan for each pancake.
4. Drop a few blueberries onto each pancake.
5. Cook until bubbles form on the surface, then flip and cook the other side.
6. Serve warm with additional blueberries on top.

Nutritional Values: Calories: 300 kcal, Protein: 10g, Fiber: 6g, Omega-3 fatty acids: 0.3g

Overnight Oats with Nuts and Berries

Ingredients:

- 1/2 cup oats
- 1 cup almond milk
- 1 tablespoon chia seeds
- 1/2 cup mixed berries (strawberries, blueberries, raspberries)
- 2 tablespoons mixed nuts (walnuts, almonds, pecans)
- 1 tablespoon honey

Steps:

1. In a jar, combine the oats, almond milk, and chia seeds.
2. Cover and refrigerate overnight.
3. In the morning, top with mixed berries, mixed nuts, and drizzle with honey.
4. Stir to combine and serve.

Nutritional Values: Calories: 350 kcal, Protein: 10g, Fiber: 8g, Omega-3 fatty acids: 2.5g

Avocado and Egg Toast

Ingredients:

- 2 slices of whole grain bread
- 1 ripe avocado
- 2 large eggs
- Olive oil, salt, and pepper to taste

Steps:

1. Toast the bread until golden.
2. Cut the avocado in half, remove the pit, and scoop out the flesh. Mash it with a fork and spread it on the toasted bread.
3. Heat a small amount of olive oil in a non-stick pan over medium heat.
4. Crack the eggs into the pan and cook to your liking.
5. Place the eggs on top of the avocado toast and season with salt and pepper.
6. Serve immediately.

Nutritional Values: Calories: 400 kcal, Protein: 15g, Fiber: 10g, Omega-3 fatty acids: 1g

These recipes are designed to offer a variety of tasty and nutrient-dense meals, suitable for seniors. They are easy to prepare and packed with brain-boosting ingredients that are essential for maintaining cognitive health in seniors.

Quinoa Breakfast Bowl

Ingredients:

- 1 cup cooked quinoa
- 1/2 cup fresh berries (blueberries, strawberries, raspberries)
- 1 tablespoon honey
- 2 tablespoons chopped nuts (walnuts, almonds)
- A dash of cinnamon

Steps:

1. In a bowl, combine the cooked quinoa, fresh berries, and chopped nuts.
2. Drizzle with honey and sprinkle with a dash of cinnamon.
3. Serve immediately.

Nutritional Values: Calories: 350 kcal, Protein: 10g, Fiber: 7g, Omega-3 fatty acids: 1.5g

Baked Avocado and Egg

Ingredients:

- 1 ripe avocado
- 2 large eggs
- Salt and pepper to taste
- A sprinkle of paprika

Steps:

1. Preheat your oven to 425°F (220°C).

2. Cut the avocado in half and remove the pit. Scoop out a little bit of the flesh to make room for the egg.
3. Crack an egg into each avocado half. Season with salt, pepper, and a sprinkle of paprika.
4. Place on a baking sheet and bake for 15-20 minutes, or until the eggs are cooked to your liking.
5. Serve immediately.

Nutritional Values: Calories: 300 kcal, Protein: 12g, Fiber: 7g, Omega-3 fatty acids: 1g

Spinach and Mushroom Frittata

Ingredients:

- 4 large eggs
- 1 cup fresh spinach
- 1 cup mushrooms, sliced
- 1 tablespoon olive oil
- Salt and pepper to taste

Steps:

1. Preheat your oven to 350°F (175°C).
2. In a bowl, whisk the eggs and season with salt and pepper.
3. Heat the olive oil in an oven-safe skillet over medium heat. Add the mushrooms and cook until they start to brown.
4. Add the spinach and cook until it wilts.
5. Pour the eggs over the veggies in the skillet and cook for a couple of minutes until the edges start to set.
6. Transfer the skillet to the oven and bake for 10-15 minutes, or until the eggs are fully set.
7. Let cool for a few minutes before serving.

Nutritional Values: Calories: 300 kcal, Protein: 20g, Fiber: 2g, Omega-3 fatty acids: 0.4g

These breakfast recipes offer seniors a variety of healthy options that are rich in Omega-3 fatty acids, fiber, and protein. Each recipe is simple to prepare and features brain-boosting ingredients to support cognitive health.

Tropical Fruit Salad with Chia Seeds

Ingredients:

- 2 cups of mixed tropical fruits (mango, pineapple, kiwi, banana)
- 1 tablespoon chia seeds
- 1 tablespoon honey
- A splash of lime juice

Steps:

1. Chop the fruits into bite-sized pieces and combine in a bowl.
2. Sprinkle with chia seeds and drizzle with honey.
3. Add a splash of lime juice and gently toss to combine.
4. Serve immediately or refrigerate for up to 2 hours before serving.

Nutritional Values: Calories: 250 kcal, Protein: 4g, Fiber: 7g, Omega-3 fatty acids: 2g

Whole Grain Cereal with Nuts and Berries

Ingredients:

- 1 cup whole grain cereal
- 1 cup almond milk
- 1/2 cup fresh berries (blueberries, strawberries, raspberries)
- 2 tablespoons mixed nuts (walnuts, almonds, pecans)

Steps:

1. In a bowl, combine the whole grain cereal and almond milk.
2. Top with fresh berries and mixed nuts.
3. Serve immediately.

Nutritional Values: Calories: 350 kcal, Protein: 9g, Fiber: 8g, Omega-3 fatty acids: 1.5g

---

Greek Yogurt with Honey and Walnuts

Ingredients:

- 1 cup Greek yogurt
- 1 tablespoon honey
- 1/4 cup walnuts, chopped
- A sprinkle of cinnamon

Steps:

1. In a bowl, combine the Greek yogurt and honey.
2. Top with chopped walnuts and a sprinkle of cinnamon.
3. Serve immediately.

Nutritional Values: Calories: 300 kcal, Protein: 18g, Fiber: 1g, Omega-3 fatty acids: 2.5g

These breakfast recipes not only cater to the tastes of seniors but also prioritize their nutritional needs. Rich in Omega-3 fatty acids, fiber, and protein, these recipes offer a variety of choices that are quick and easy to prepare, tasty, and beneficial for brain health.

Almond Butter Banana Toast

Ingredients:

- 2 slices of whole grain bread
- 2 tablespoons almond butter
- 1 banana, sliced
- A sprinkle of cinnamon

Steps:

1. Toast the bread until golden.
2. Spread the almond butter evenly over each slice.
3. Top with banana slices and a sprinkle of cinnamon.
4. Serve immediately.

Nutritional Values: Calories: 350 kcal, Protein: 12g, Fiber: 6g, Omega-3 fatty acids: 0.2g

---

Berry Smoothie Bowl

Ingredients:

- 1 cup mixed berries (blueberries, strawberries, raspberries)
- 1/2 banana
- 1 cup Greek yogurt
- 1 tablespoon honey
- Toppings: granola, chia seeds, fresh berries

Steps:

1. In a blender, combine the mixed berries, banana, Greek yogurt, and honey. Blend until smooth.

2. Pour into a bowl and top with granola, chia seeds, and fresh berries as desired.
3. Serve immediately.

Nutritional Values: Calories: 300 kcal, Protein: 15g, Fiber: 7g, Omega-3 fatty acids: 1g

---

Baked Sweet Potato with Almond Butter

Ingredients:

- 1 medium sweet potato
- 2 tablespoons almond butter
- A sprinkle of cinnamon

Steps:

1. Preheat your oven to 400°F (200°C). Prick the sweet potato with a fork a few times and wrap it in aluminum foil.
2. Bake for 45-50 minutes, or until the sweet potato is soft and cooked through.
3. Let it cool for a few minutes, then cut it open and fluff the inside with a fork.
4. Drizzle with almond butter and a sprinkle of cinnamon.
5. Serve warm.

Nutritional Values: Calories: 350 kcal, Protein: 8g, Fiber: 6g, Omega-3 fatty acids: 0.2g

These easy-to-prepare recipes are perfect for seniors looking to maintain a brain-healthy diet. Each recipe is full of beneficial nutrients like fiber, protein, and omega-3 fatty acids that support cognitive function and overall health. The diverse flavors and textures ensure that there's a delicious and nutritious breakfast option for every preference.

Lunch

Grilled Salmon with Quinoa and Veggies

Ingredients:

- 1 salmon fillet
- 1 tablespoon olive oil
- Salt and pepper to taste
- 1/2 cup cooked quinoa
- 1 cup mixed veggies (broccoli, bell pepper, carrot)
- Lemon slices for serving

Steps:

1. Preheat your grill or grill pan to medium heat.
2. Brush the salmon with olive oil and season with salt and pepper.
3. Grill the salmon for about 4-5 minutes on each side, or until it's cooked to your desired level.
4. In the meantime, steam the mixed veggies until they're tender.
5. Serve the grilled salmon with the cooked quinoa and steamed veggies. Garnish with lemon slices.

Nutritional Values: Calories: 500 kcal, Protein: 35g, Fiber: 6g, Omega-3 fatty acids: 3g

---

Avocado and Chickpea Salad

Ingredients:

- 1 ripe avocado, diced

- 1 cup canned chickpeas, drained and rinsed
- 1/2 red onion, diced
- 1 cup cherry tomatoes, halved
- 1 tablespoon olive oil
- Juice of 1 lemon
- Salt and pepper to taste

Steps:

1. In a large bowl, combine the avocado, chickpeas, red onion, and cherry tomatoes.
2. Drizzle with olive oil and lemon juice. Season with salt and pepper.
3. Gently toss until everything is well mixed.
4. Serve immediately or refrigerate for up to 2 hours before serving.

Nutritional Values: Calories: 400 kcal, Protein: 10g, Fiber: 12g, Omega-3 fatty acids: 1g

Spinach and Mushroom Whole Wheat Pasta

Ingredients:

- 2 cups whole wheat pasta
- 2 cups fresh spinach
- 1 cup mushrooms, sliced
- 2 tablespoons olive oil
- 2 cloves garlic, minced
- Salt and pepper to taste
- Parmesan cheese for serving (optional)

Steps:

1. Cook the pasta according to package instructions until al dente.

2. While the pasta is cooking, heat the olive oil in a large skillet over medium heat. Add the garlic and cook until fragrant.
3. Add the mushrooms and cook until they're browned. Add the spinach and cook until it wilts.
4. Drain the pasta and add it to the skillet. Toss until everything is well mixed. Season with salt and pepper.
5. Serve warm with a sprinkle of Parmesan cheese, if desired.

Nutritional Values: Calories: 500 kcal, Protein: 15g, Fiber: 8g, Omega-3 fatty acids: 0.3g

These lunch recipes are simple to prepare and packed with ingredients that support brain health, such as Omega-3 fatty acids, fiber, and lean proteins. They provide a variety of tastes and textures, ensuring that seniors can enjoy a different, delicious, and nutritious meal every day.

Grilled Chicken with Avocado Salsa

Ingredients:

- 1 chicken breast
- 1 tablespoon olive oil
- Salt and pepper to taste
- 1 ripe avocado, diced
- 1 tomato, diced
- 1/4 red onion, finely chopped
- Juice of 1 lime
- A handful of fresh cilantro, chopped

Steps:

1. Preheat your grill or grill pan to medium heat.
2. Brush the chicken with olive oil and season with salt and pepper. Grill for about 5-7 minutes on each side, or until it's cooked through.

3. In a bowl, combine the avocado, tomato, red onion, lime juice, and cilantro. Season with salt and pepper and stir until well mixed.
4. Serve the grilled chicken with the avocado salsa on top.

Nutritional Values: Calories: 400 kcal, Protein: 30g, Fiber: 7g, Omega-3 fatty acids: 0.3g

Quinoa Stuffed Bell Peppers

Ingredients:

- 2 bell peppers, halved and seeds removed
- 1 cup cooked quinoa
- 1/2 cup black beans, drained and rinsed
- 1/2 cup corn kernels
- 1/2 cup diced tomatoes
- 1/2 cup shredded cheese
- Salt and pepper to taste

Steps:

1. Preheat your oven to 375°F (190°C).
2. In a large bowl, combine the quinoa, black beans, corn, tomatoes, and cheese. Season with salt and pepper and stir until well mixed.
3. Spoon the quinoa mixture into the bell pepper halves and place them on a baking sheet.
4. Bake for about 25-30 minutes, or until the peppers are tender and the cheese is melted.
5. Serve warm.

Nutritional Values: Calories: 350 kcal, Protein: 12g, Fiber: 7g, Omega-3 fatty acids: 0.2g

Mediterranean Tuna Salad

Ingredients:

- 2 cans of tuna, drained
- 1/2 cucumber, diced
- 1/2 red onion, finely chopped
- 1/2 cup cherry tomatoes, halved
- 1/4 cup black olives, sliced
- 1 tablespoon olive oil
- Juice of 1 lemon
- Salt and pepper to taste

Steps:

1. In a large bowl, combine the tuna, cucumber, red onion, cherry tomatoes, and black olives.
2. Drizzle with olive oil and lemon juice. Season with salt and pepper.
3. Gently toss until everything is well mixed.
4. Serve immediately or refrigerate for up to 2 hours before serving.

Nutritional Values: Calories: 300 kcal, Protein: 25g, Fiber: 2g, Omega-3 fatty acids: 2.5g

These lunch recipes focus on the use of brain-boosting ingredients, rich in Omega-3 fatty acids, fiber, and lean proteins. They're simple to prepare, ensuring that seniors can enjoy a delicious and nutritious meal every day.

Baked Salmon with Sweet Potato Fries

Ingredients:

- 1 salmon fillet
- 1 tablespoon olive oil
- Salt and pepper to taste
- 1 large sweet potato
- 2 tablespoons coconut oil
- A sprinkle of paprika

Steps:

1. Preheat your oven to 400°F (200°C).
2. Brush the salmon with olive oil and season with salt and pepper. Place it on a baking sheet and bake for 15-20 minutes, or until it's cooked to your desired level.
3. While the salmon is baking, cut the sweet potato into fries. Toss with coconut oil, salt, pepper, and paprika.
4. Spread the fries on a separate baking sheet and bake for about 30 minutes, flipping halfway through, until they're golden and crispy.
5. Serve the baked salmon with the sweet potato fries.

Nutritional Values: Calories: 550 kcal, Protein: 35g, Fiber: 5g, Omega-3 fatty acids: 3g

---

Quinoa and Vegetable Stir-Fry

Ingredients:

- 1 cup cooked quinoa
- 2 cups mixed vegetables (broccoli, bell pepper, carrots, peas)
- 1 tablespoon olive oil
- 2 tablespoons low-sodium soy sauce

- 1 clove garlic, minced
- Salt and pepper to taste

Steps:

1. Heat the olive oil in a large skillet or wok over medium heat. Add the garlic and cook until fragrant.
2. Add the mixed vegetables and stir-fry until they're tender-crisp.
3. Add the cooked quinoa to the skillet. Pour the soy sauce over everything and stir until well mixed.
4. Season with salt and pepper. Serve warm.

Nutritional Values: Calories: 350 kcal, Protein: 10g, Fiber: 7g, Omega-3 fatty acids: 0.3g

---

Lentil and Veggie Soup

Ingredients:

- 1 cup green lentils
- 4 cups vegetable broth
- 1 onion, chopped
- 2 carrots, chopped
- 2 celery stalks, chopped
- 1 clove garlic, minced
- 1 tablespoon olive oil
- Salt and pepper to taste

Steps:

1. In a large pot, heat the olive oil over medium heat. Add the onion, carrots, and celery and cook until they start to soften.
2. Add the garlic and cook for another minute until fragrant.
3. Add the lentils and vegetable broth to the pot. Bring to a boil, then reduce the heat and simmer for about 30-40 minutes, or until the lentils are tender.

4. Season with salt and pepper. Serve warm.

Nutritional Values: Calories: 400 kcal, Protein: 20g, Fiber: 16g, Omega-3 fatty acids: 0.2g

These lunch recipes not only provide a burst of flavor but also ensure that seniors are getting the nutrients they need for optimal brain health. Each dish is filled with Omega-3 fatty acids, fiber, and lean proteins, all key elements of a brain-healthy diet.

Turmeric Chicken Salad

Ingredients:

- 2 cups shredded chicken
- 1/4 cup Greek yogurt
- 1/2 teaspoon turmeric
- 1/2 teaspoon black pepper
- 1/4 cup sliced almonds
- 1 apple, chopped
- 2 celery stalks, chopped
- Salt to taste

Steps:

1. In a large bowl, mix Greek yogurt, turmeric, black pepper, and salt.
2. Add the shredded chicken, sliced almonds, chopped apple, and celery to the bowl. Stir until well combined.
3. Refrigerate for 1 hour before serving to allow flavors to meld.

Nutritional Values: Calories: 450 kcal, Protein: 45g, Fiber: 6g, Omega-3 fatty acids: 0.2g

Sweet Potato and Black Bean Buddha Bowl

Ingredients:

- 1 sweet potato, cubed
- 1 cup black beans, rinsed and drained
- 1 cup cooked quinoa
- 2 cups spinach
- 1 tablespoon olive oil
- Salt and pepper to taste
- Dressing: 2 tablespoons tahini, juice of 1 lemon, 1 tablespoon honey

Steps:

1. Preheat your oven to 400°F (200°C). Toss the sweet potato cubes with olive oil, salt, and pepper, and spread them on a baking sheet. Bake for about 20-25 minutes, or until they're tender and golden.
2. Prepare the dressing by whisking together tahini, lemon juice, and honey.
3. Assemble your bowl with a base of spinach, followed by quinoa, black beans, and roasted sweet potato. Drizzle with the tahini dressing before serving.

Nutritional Values: Calories: 500 kcal, Protein: 15g, Fiber: 15g, Omega-3 fatty acids: 0.5g

---

Smashed Chickpea and Avocado Sandwich

Ingredients:

- 1 can chickpeas, rinsed and drained
- 1 ripe avocado
- Juice of 1/2 lemon

- 2 slices of whole grain bread
- A handful of fresh spinach
- Salt and pepper to taste

Steps:

1. In a bowl, mash the chickpeas and avocado together. Add the lemon juice, salt, and pepper, and mix until well combined.
2. Spread the chickpea and avocado mixture onto one slice of bread. Top with fresh spinach.
3. Cover with the second slice of bread and cut in half.
4. Serve immediately.

Nutritional Values: Calories: 400 kcal, Protein: 15g, Fiber: 12g, Omega-3 fatty acids: 1g

These lunch recipes are easy to prepare and deliver nutrients that are essential for the brain's health, such as Omega-3 fatty acids, fiber, and lean proteins. The variety in flavors and textures ensure a delightful and nutritious meal every time.

Roasted Beet and Goat Cheese Salad

Ingredients:

- 2 medium beets
- 4 cups mixed greens
- 1/4 cup goat cheese, crumbled
- 1/4 cup walnuts, chopped
- 2 tablespoons balsamic vinaigrette

Steps:

1. Preheat your oven to 400°F (200°C). Wrap the beets in aluminum foil and roast for about 50-60 minutes, or until tender. Once cooled, peel and slice the beets.
2. Assemble your salad with a base of mixed greens, followed by the roasted beets, crumbled goat cheese, and chopped walnuts.
3. Drizzle with balsamic vinaigrette before serving.

Nutritional Values: Calories: 300 kcal, Protein: 8g, Fiber: 6g, Omega-3 fatty acids: 1g

Spinach and Feta Stuffed Chicken Breast

Ingredients:

- 2 chicken breasts
- 1 cup fresh spinach, chopped
- 1/4 cup feta cheese, crumbled
- 1 tablespoon olive oil
- Salt and pepper to taste

Steps:

1. Preheat your oven to 375°F (190°C). Cut a slit into the side of each chicken breast to create a pocket.
2. Stuff the pockets with the chopped spinach and crumbled feta. Secure with toothpicks if necessary.
3. Brush the chicken with olive oil and season with salt and pepper. Place on a baking sheet and bake for about 25-30 minutes, or until the chicken is cooked through.
4. Let it rest for a few minutes before serving.

Nutritional Values: Calories: 400 kcal, Protein: 55g, Fiber: 1g, Omega-3 fatty acids: 0.5g

Lentil Stuffed Bell Peppers

Ingredients:

- 2 bell peppers, halved and seeds removed
- 1 cup cooked lentils
- 1/2 onion, chopped
- 1 clove garlic, minced
- 1 tablespoon olive oil
- Salt and pepper to taste
- 1/4 cup shredded cheese

Steps:

1. Preheat your oven to 375°F (190°C).
2. In a skillet, heat the olive oil over medium heat. Add the onion and garlic and sauté until soft.
3. Add the cooked lentils to the skillet and stir to combine. Season with salt and pepper.
4. Spoon the lentil mixture into the bell pepper halves. Sprinkle with shredded cheese.
5. Place on a baking sheet and bake for about 25-30 minutes, or until the peppers are tender and the cheese is melted.
6. Serve warm.

Nutritional Values: Calories: 350 kcal, Protein: 20g, Fiber: 10g, Omega-3 fatty acids: 0.3g

These nutritious lunch recipes are perfect for seniors, packed with brain-boosting ingredients such as Omega-3 fatty acids, fiber, and lean proteins. They offer a variety of flavors to keep meals exciting and enjoyable.

Baked Cod with Lemon and Dill

Ingredients:

- 2 cod fillets
- 2 tablespoons olive oil
- Juice of 1 lemon
- 1 teaspoon fresh dill, chopped
- Salt and pepper to taste

Steps:

1. Preheat your oven to 400°F (200°C).
2. Place the cod fillets on a baking sheet. Drizzle with olive oil and lemon juice, then season with salt, pepper, and dill.
3. Bake for 12-15 minutes, or until the fish is flaky and cooked through.
4. Serve immediately.

Nutritional Values: Calories: 300 kcal, Protein: 40g, Fiber: 0g, Omega-3 fatty acids: 2g

Quinoa, Black Bean, and Avocado Salad

Ingredients:

- 2 cups cooked quinoa
- 1 cup black beans, rinsed and drained
- 1 ripe avocado, diced
- 1/2 cup cherry tomatoes, halved
- 1/4 cup red onion, finely chopped
- Juice of 1 lime
- 1 tablespoon olive oil
- Salt and pepper to taste

Steps:

1. In a large bowl, combine the quinoa, black beans, avocado, cherry tomatoes, and red onion.
2. Drizzle with lime juice and olive oil. Season with salt and pepper.
3. Toss until everything is well mixed. Serve immediately or refrigerate until ready to serve.

Nutritional Values: Calories: 400 kcal, Protein: 15g, Fiber: 10g, Omega-3 fatty acids: 1.2g

Veggie Hummus Wrap

Ingredients:

- 2 whole grain wraps
- 1/2 cup hummus
- 1 carrot, peeled and shredded
- 1/2 cucumber, thinly sliced
- 1 bell pepper, thinly sliced
- 2 cups spinach leaves

Steps:

1. Spread the hummus evenly on the whole grain wraps.
2. Top with shredded carrot, sliced cucumber, sliced bell pepper, and spinach leaves.
3. Roll the wrap tightly, then cut in half.
4. Serve immediately or wrap in foil and refrigerate until ready to serve.

Nutritional Values: Calories: 300 kcal, Protein: 10g, Fiber: 8g, Omega-3 fatty acids: 0.3g

These lunch recipes are designed to provide a delicious and nutritious meal for seniors. Each recipe uses brain-boosting ingredients that are high in Omega-3 fatty acids, fiber, and lean proteins. These simple, wholesome recipes offer a variety of flavors, ensuring a satisfying meal every day.

Tuna Salad with Greek Yogurt Dressing

Ingredients:

- 1 can of tuna in water, drained
- 1/4 cup Greek yogurt
- 1/4 cup celery, chopped
- 1/4 cup red onion, finely chopped
- 2 tablespoons fresh parsley, chopped
- Salt and pepper to taste
- 2 cups mixed salad greens

Steps:

1. In a bowl, combine the drained tuna, Greek yogurt, celery, red onion, and parsley. Season with salt and pepper.
2. Place the mixed salad greens on a plate and top with the tuna salad.
3. Serve immediately.

Nutritional Values: Calories: 300 kcal, Protein: 40g, Fiber: 2g, Omega-3 fatty acids: 2.5g

Lentil and Sweet Potato Shepherd's Pie

Ingredients:

- 1 cup green lentils, cooked
- 2 sweet potatoes, cooked and mashed
- 1 onion, chopped
- 2 cloves garlic, minced
- 2 carrots, diced
- 1 cup peas
- 1 tablespoon olive oil
- Salt and pepper to taste

Steps:

1. Preheat your oven to 375°F (190°C).
2. In a skillet, heat the olive oil over medium heat. Add the onion, garlic, and carrots and sauté until soft.
3. Stir in the peas and cooked lentils, then season with salt and pepper.
4. Transfer the lentil mixture to a baking dish and top with the mashed sweet potatoes.
5. Bake for 20-25 minutes, or until the top is golden.
6. Serve warm.

Nutritional Values: Calories: 400 kcal, Protein: 20g, Fiber: 15g, Omega-3 fatty acids: 0.3g

---

Mediterranean Chickpea Salad

Ingredients:

- 2 cups chickpeas, rinsed and drained
- 1 cucumber, diced
- 1 bell pepper, diced
- 1/4 cup Kalamata olives, sliced
- 1/4 cup feta cheese, crumbled
- Dressing: Juice of 1 lemon, 2 tablespoons olive oil, 1 clove garlic minced, Salt and pepper to taste

Steps:

1. In a large bowl, combine the chickpeas, cucumber, bell pepper, Kalamata olives, and feta cheese.
2. Prepare the dressing by whisking together the lemon juice, olive oil, and minced garlic. Season with salt and pepper.
3. Drizzle the dressing over the salad and toss until everything is well mixed.
4. Serve immediately or refrigerate until ready to serve.

Nutritional Values: Calories: 400 kcal, Protein: 14g, Fiber: 10g, Omega-3 fatty acids: 0.6g

These brain-healthy lunch recipes for seniors feature nutrient-dense foods that support cognitive health. Each meal offers a unique combination of flavors and textures to keep seniors looking forward to lunchtime.

Baked Salmon with Quinoa and Broccoli

Ingredients:

- 2 salmon fillets
- 1 cup quinoa, cooked
- 2 cups broccoli florets
- 1 tablespoon olive oil
- Salt and pepper to taste
- Lemon slices for garnish

Steps:

1. Preheat your oven to 400°F (200°C).
2. Place the salmon fillets on a baking sheet, drizzle with olive oil and season with salt and pepper. Bake for 12-15 minutes, or until the salmon is cooked through.

3. In the meantime, steam the broccoli florets until tender.
4. Serve the baked salmon with cooked quinoa and steamed broccoli. Garnish with lemon slices.

Nutritional Values: Calories: 500 kcal, Protein: 45g, Fiber: 6g, Omega-3 fatty acids: 2g

Stuffed Portobello Mushrooms

Ingredients:

- 4 large portobello mushrooms, stems and gills removed
- 1 cup spinach, chopped
- 1/2 cup feta cheese, crumbled
- 1/2 cup cherry tomatoes, halved
- 1 tablespoon olive oil
- Salt and pepper to taste

Steps:

1. Preheat your oven to 375°F (190°C).
2. Brush the mushrooms with olive oil and place them on a baking sheet.
3. In a bowl, combine the spinach, feta cheese, and cherry tomatoes. Season with salt and pepper.
4. Spoon the mixture into the mushroom caps.
5. Bake for 15-20 minutes, or until the mushrooms are tender and the cheese is melted.
6. Serve warm.

Nutritional Values: Calories: 250 kcal, Protein: 10g, Fiber: 3g, Omega-3 fatty acids: 0.5g

Greek Yogurt Chicken Salad

Ingredients:

- 2 cups shredded chicken
- 1/2 cup Greek yogurt
- 1 apple, diced
- 1/4 cup walnuts, chopped
- 1/4 cup celery, chopped
- Salt and pepper to taste

Steps:

1. In a large bowl, combine the shredded chicken, Greek yogurt, diced apple, chopped walnuts, and celery. Season with salt and pepper.
2. Mix until well combined.
3. Serve immediately, or refrigerate until ready to serve.

Nutritional Values: Calories: 400 kcal, Protein: 40g, Fiber: 5g, Omega-3 fatty acids: 1g

These lunch recipes are designed to be both delicious and beneficial for seniors' brain health. They offer a balance of proteins, fiber, and Omega-3 fatty acids, all of which are essential for maintaining cognitive function. Enjoy these varied, nutrient-rich meals for a satisfying and brain-healthy lunch.

Dinner

Oven-Baked Rosemary Chicken

Ingredients:

- 2 chicken breasts
- 1 tablespoon olive oil
- 1 tablespoon fresh rosemary, chopped
- Salt and pepper to taste
- 2 cups mixed vegetables of your choice

Steps:

1. Preheat your oven to 375°F (190°C).
2. Rub the chicken breasts with olive oil, rosemary, salt, and pepper. Place on a baking sheet.
3. Roast in the oven for 25-30 minutes, or until the chicken is cooked through.
4. Steam or roast your choice of vegetables to serve alongside the chicken.

Nutritional Values: Calories: 400 kcal, Protein: 55g, Fiber: 5g, Omega-3 fatty acids: 0.5g

---

Tofu and Broccoli Stir-Fry

Ingredients:

- 1 block firm tofu, cubed
- 2 cups broccoli florets
- 1 bell pepper, sliced

- 2 tablespoons soy sauce
- 1 tablespoon sesame oil
- 1 tablespoon olive oil
- 1 garlic clove, minced

Steps:

1. Heat the olive oil in a large skillet or wok over medium heat.
2. Add the tofu cubes and cook until they are golden brown on all sides. Remove from the skillet and set aside.
3. In the same skillet, add the broccoli and bell pepper. Sauté until tender.
4. Add the tofu back to the skillet. Stir in the soy sauce, sesame oil, and minced garlic.
5. Cook for another 2-3 minutes, then serve hot.

Nutritional Values: Calories: 350 kcal, Protein: 20g, Fiber: 5g, Omega-3 fatty acids: 1g

---

Lemon Garlic Shrimp and Quinoa

Ingredients:

- 2 cups cooked quinoa
- 1 pound shrimp, peeled and deveined
- 2 tablespoons olive oil
- 4 cloves garlic, minced
- Juice of 1 lemon
- Salt and pepper to taste
- Fresh parsley for garnish

Steps:

1. Heat the olive oil in a large skillet over medium heat.
2. Add the shrimp and cook until they turn pink, about 2-3 minutes per side. Remove from the skillet and set aside.

3. In the same skillet, add the garlic and cook until fragrant.
4. Stir in the cooked quinoa and shrimp. Drizzle with lemon juice and season with salt and pepper.
5. Cook for another 2-3 minutes, then garnish with fresh parsley before serving.

Nutritional Values: Calories: 450 kcal, Protein: 40g, Fiber: 5g, Omega-3 fatty acids: 1.5g

These dinner recipes for seniors incorporate a variety of brain-boosting ingredients such as lean proteins, Omega-3 fatty acids, and vegetables. Each recipe is designed to be easy to prepare and delicious to enjoy, promoting both physical health and mental well-being.

Baked Sweet Potato with Spinach and Feta

Ingredients:

- 2 large sweet potatoes
- 2 cups spinach, chopped
- 1/2 cup feta cheese, crumbled
- 1 tablespoon olive oil
- Salt and pepper to taste

Steps:

1. Preheat your oven to 400°F (200°C).
2. Pierce the sweet potatoes with a fork and place them on a baking sheet. Bake for 45-50 minutes, or until tender.
3. While the sweet potatoes are baking, heat the olive oil in a skillet over medium heat. Add the spinach and cook until wilted.
4. Cut the baked sweet potatoes in half and top with the wilted spinach and crumbled feta cheese. Season with salt and pepper.
5. Serve warm.

Nutritional Values: Calories: 300 kcal, Protein: 10g, Fiber: 6g, Omega-3 fatty acids: 0.3g

---

Brown Rice and Black Bean Bowl

Ingredients:

- 2 cups cooked brown rice
- 1 cup black beans, rinsed and drained
- 1 avocado, sliced
- 1 tomato, diced
- 1/4 cup red onion, finely chopped
- 1/4 cup fresh cilantro, chopped
- Juice of 1 lime
- 1 tablespoon olive oil
- Salt and pepper to taste

Steps:

1. In a large bowl, combine the cooked brown rice, black beans, avocado slices, diced tomato, and red onion.
2. Drizzle with lime juice and olive oil. Season with salt and pepper.
3. Garnish with fresh cilantro before serving.

Nutritional Values: Calories: 400 kcal, Protein: 12g, Fiber: 10g, Omega-3 fatty acids: 1.2g

---

Grilled Salmon with Asparagus and Quinoa

Ingredients:

- 2 salmon fillets
- 2 cups asparagus, ends trimmed
- 1 cup cooked quinoa
- 1 tablespoon olive oil
- Salt and pepper to taste
- Lemon slices for garnish

Steps:

1. Preheat your grill or grill pan over medium-high heat.
2. Brush the salmon fillets and asparagus with olive oil, then season with salt and pepper.
3. Grill the salmon for 4-5 minutes on each side, or until cooked to your desired doneness. Grill the asparagus until tender.
4. Serve the grilled salmon and asparagus with cooked quinoa. Garnish with lemon slices.

Nutritional Values: Calories: 500 kcal, Protein: 45g, Fiber: 6g, Omega-3 fatty acids: 2g

These brain-healthy dinner recipes for seniors are packed with nutrient-rich foods to support overall health and cognitive function. With an array of flavors and textures, these recipes make dinner time a delightful and nourishing experience.

Baked Cod with Tomato and Olive Sauce

Ingredients:

- 2 cod fillets
- 1 cup cherry tomatoes, halved
- 1/2 cup Kalamata olives, pitted and sliced
- 1/4 cup fresh basil, chopped
- 2 tablespoons olive oil
- Salt and pepper to taste

Steps:

1. Preheat your oven to 400°F (200°C).
2. Arrange the cod fillets in a baking dish. Scatter the cherry tomatoes and olives around the fish.
3. Drizzle with olive oil, then season with salt and pepper.
4. Bake for 15-20 minutes, or until the fish is flaky and cooked through.
5. Garnish with fresh basil before serving.

Nutritional Values: Calories: 350 kcal, Protein: 35g, Fiber: 3g, Omega-3 fatty acids: 1g

---

Quinoa Salad with Avocado and Almonds

Ingredients:

- 2 cups cooked quinoa
- 1 avocado, cubed
- 1/2 cup roasted almonds, chopped
- 1 bell pepper, diced
- 2 tablespoons olive oil
- Juice of 1 lemon
- Salt and pepper to taste

Steps:

1. In a large bowl, combine the cooked quinoa, avocado, almonds, and bell pepper.
2. In a small bowl, whisk together the olive oil and lemon juice. Season with salt and pepper.
3. Pour the dressing over the salad and toss until everything is well coated.
4. Serve immediately or refrigerate until ready to serve.

Nutritional Values: Calories: 450 kcal, Protein: 15g, Fiber: 10g, Omega-3 fatty acids: 1g

Oven-Roasted Brussels Sprouts with Walnuts

Ingredients:

- 2 cups Brussels sprouts, trimmed and halved
- 1/2 cup walnuts, chopped
- 2 tablespoons olive oil
- Salt and pepper to taste

Steps:

1. Preheat your oven to 400°F (200°C).
2. Arrange the Brussels sprouts on a baking sheet. Drizzle with olive oil and season with salt and pepper.
3. Roast for 15-20 minutes, or until the Brussels sprouts are tender and golden. Halfway through, scatter the chopped walnuts on the baking sheet.
4. Serve warm.

Nutritional Values: Calories: 300 kcal, Protein: 10g, Fiber: 7g, Omega-3 fatty acids: 1.5g

These dinner recipes are packed with nutrients crucial for senior health, particularly brain health. They feature lean proteins, wholesome grains, and vegetables, all prepared in a way that's both delicious and beneficial to the body and mind. Enjoy these meals to round off a day of nourishing, brain-healthy eating.

Baked Salmon with Dill and Lemon

Ingredients:

- 2 salmon fillets
- 1 tablespoon olive oil
- Juice of 1 lemon
- 1 tablespoon fresh dill, chopped
- Salt and pepper to taste

Steps:

1. Preheat your oven to 375°F (190°C).
2. Place the salmon fillets on a baking sheet. Drizzle with olive oil and lemon juice, then sprinkle with dill, salt, and pepper.
3. Bake for 15-20 minutes, or until the salmon is cooked through.
4. Serve hot.

Nutritional Values: Calories: 400 kcal, Protein: 35g, Fiber: 0g, Omega-3 fatty acids: 2g

Barley and Mushroom Risotto

Ingredients:

- 1 cup pearl barley
- 2 cups vegetable broth

- 1 cup mushrooms, sliced
- 1 onion, diced
- 2 cloves garlic, minced
- 2 tablespoons olive oil
- Salt and pepper to taste

Steps:

1. In a large pot, heat the olive oil over medium heat. Add the onion and garlic, cooking until they are soft and fragrant.
2. Add the mushrooms and continue cooking until they are tender.
3. Stir in the barley, then add the vegetable broth. Bring to a boil, then reduce the heat and simmer for 40-45 minutes, or until the barley is tender.
4. Season with salt and pepper, then serve hot.

Nutritional Values: Calories: 350 kcal, Protein: 10g, Fiber: 15g, Omega-3 fatty acids: 0.5g

Beet and Goat Cheese Salad

Ingredients:

- 4 beets, roasted and sliced
- 2 cups mixed greens
- 1/2 cup goat cheese, crumbled
- 1/4 cup walnuts, chopped
- 2 tablespoons balsamic vinegar
- 1 tablespoon olive oil
- Salt and pepper to taste

Steps:

1. In a large bowl, combine the mixed greens, sliced beets, goat cheese, and walnuts.

2. Drizzle with balsamic vinegar and olive oil, then season with salt and pepper.
3. Toss the salad until everything is well coated, then serve.

Nutritional Values: Calories: 300 kcal, Protein: 10g, Fiber: 5g, Omega-3 fatty acids: 1g

These dinner recipes for seniors are designed to be both delicious and beneficial for brain health. They feature a variety of nutrient-dense ingredients, including lean protein, whole grains, and fresh vegetables, all of which contribute to overall health and cognitive function.

Baked Tilapia with Lemon and Herbs

Ingredients:

- 2 tilapia fillets
- Juice of 1 lemon
- 2 tablespoons fresh parsley, chopped
- 1 tablespoon olive oil
- Salt and pepper to taste

Steps:

1. Preheat your oven to 400°F (200°C).
2. Place the tilapia fillets on a baking sheet. Drizzle with lemon juice and olive oil, then sprinkle with parsley, salt, and pepper.
3. Bake for 15-20 minutes, or until the fish is flaky and cooked through.
4. Serve hot.

Nutritional Values: Calories: 300 kcal, Protein: 28g, Fiber: 0g, Omega-3 fatty acids: 0.7g

Chickpea and Vegetable Stir Fry

Ingredients:

- 1 can chickpeas, rinsed and drained
- 1 bell pepper, sliced
- 1 zucchini, sliced
- 1 onion, sliced
- 2 cloves garlic, minced
- 2 tablespoons olive oil
- Salt and pepper to taste

Steps:

1. Heat the olive oil in a large skillet over medium heat. Add the onion and garlic, cooking until they are soft and fragrant.
2. Add the bell pepper and zucchini, cooking until they are tender.
3. Stir in the chickpeas and continue to cook for another 5 minutes.
4. Season with salt and pepper, then serve hot.

Nutritional Values: Calories: 350 kcal, Protein: 14g, Fiber: 10g, Omega-3 fatty acids: 0.3g

---

Spinach and Tomato Frittata

Ingredients:

- 6 eggs
- 2 cups spinach, chopped
- 1 cup cherry tomatoes, halved
- 1/2 cup feta cheese, crumbled
- 1 tablespoon olive oil
- Salt and pepper to taste

Steps:

1. Preheat your oven to 375°F (190°C).
2. In a large bowl, beat the eggs. Stir in the spinach, cherry tomatoes, and feta cheese. Season with salt and pepper.
3. Heat the olive oil in an oven-safe skillet over medium heat. Pour in the egg mixture.
4. Cook for 5-7 minutes, or until the edges are set.
5. Transfer the skillet to the oven and bake for 10-15 minutes, or until the frittata is set in the middle.
6. Serve hot.

Nutritional Values: Calories: 200 kcal, Protein: 14g, Fiber: 2g, Omega-3 fatty acids: 0.5g

These dinner recipes are tailored for seniors, with a focus on promoting brain health. They are simple, flavorful, and packed with nutrients that support cognitive function and overall health. Enjoy these meals as part of a balanced, brain-healthy diet.

Broccoli and Cheddar Soup

Ingredients:

- 2 cups broccoli, chopped
- 1 onion, diced
- 2 cloves garlic, minced
- 1 cup cheddar cheese, grated
- 4 cups vegetable broth
- 2 tablespoons olive oil
- Salt and pepper to taste

Steps:

1. Heat the olive oil in a large pot over medium heat. Add the onion and garlic, cooking until they are soft and fragrant.

2. Add the broccoli and vegetable broth. Bring to a boil, then reduce the heat and simmer for 20-25 minutes, or until the broccoli is tender.
3. Use an immersion blender to puree the soup until smooth. Alternatively, you can transfer the soup to a countertop blender to puree it.
4. Stir in the cheddar cheese until it is melted and incorporated.
5. Season with salt and pepper, then serve hot.

Nutritional Values: Calories: 300 kcal, Protein: 10g, Fiber: 3g, Omega-3 fatty acids: 0.3g

Quinoa Stuffed Bell Peppers

Ingredients:

- 4 bell peppers, tops removed and seeds scooped out
- 2 cups cooked quinoa
- 1 cup black beans, rinsed and drained
- 1 cup corn kernels
- 1 cup tomato salsa
- 1 cup cheddar cheese, grated
- 1 tablespoon olive oil
- Salt and pepper to taste

Steps:

1. Preheat your oven to 375°F (190°C).
2. In a large bowl, combine the cooked quinoa, black beans, corn, salsa, and half of the cheddar cheese. Season with salt and pepper.
3. Spoon the quinoa mixture into the bell peppers, filling them to the top. Place the stuffed bell peppers in a baking dish.
4. Drizzle with olive oil and sprinkle with the remaining cheddar cheese.

5. Bake for 25-30 minutes, or until the bell peppers are tender and the cheese is melted and golden.
6. Serve hot.

Nutritional Values: Calories: 400 kcal, Protein: 15g, Fiber: 10g, Omega-3 fatty acids: 0.3g

---

Tofu Stir Fry with Mixed Vegetables

Ingredients:

- 1 package firm tofu, drained and cubed
- 2 cups mixed vegetables (e.g., bell pepper, broccoli, snap peas, carrots), chopped
- 2 cloves garlic, minced
- 2 tablespoons soy sauce
- 1 tablespoon sesame oil
- 1 tablespoon olive oil

Steps:

1. Heat the olive oil in a large skillet over medium heat. Add the tofu cubes and cook until they are golden and crispy.
2. Remove the tofu from the skillet and set aside.
3. In the same skillet, add the mixed vegetables and garlic. Cook until the vegetables are tender.
4. Add the tofu back into the skillet. Drizzle with soy sauce and sesame oil, then toss to coat everything in the sauce.
5. Serve hot.

Nutritional Values: Calories: 300 kcal, Protein: 20g, Fiber: 6g, Omega-3 fatty acids: 0.3g

These dinner recipes are easy to prepare, tasty, and designed to promote brain health in seniors. They incorporate a variety of ingredients that are rich in nutrients necessary for maintaining cognitive function, making them a great addition to any senior's diet.

Lentil and Spinach Dal

Ingredients:

- 1 cup red lentils, rinsed
- 2 cups fresh spinach, chopped
- 1 onion, diced
- 2 cloves garlic, minced
- 1 tablespoon curry powder
- 1 teaspoon turmeric
- 4 cups vegetable broth
- 1 tablespoon olive oil
- Salt and pepper to taste

Steps:

1. Heat the olive oil in a large pot over medium heat. Add the onion and garlic, cooking until they are soft and fragrant.
2. Stir in the curry powder and turmeric, then add the red lentils and vegetable broth.
3. Bring the mixture to a boil, then reduce the heat and simmer for 20-25 minutes, or until the lentils are tender.
4. Stir in the chopped spinach until it is wilted.
5. Season with salt and pepper, then serve hot.

Nutritional Values: Calories: 300 kcal, Protein: 20g, Fiber: 10g, Omega-3 fatty acids: 0.3g

Baked Cod with Olives and Tomatoes

Ingredients:

- 2 cod fillets
- 1 cup cherry tomatoes, halved
- 1/2 cup kalamata olives, pitted and sliced
- 2 tablespoons olive oil
- Juice of 1 lemon
- Salt and pepper to taste

Steps:

1. Preheat your oven to 400°F (200°C).
2. Place the cod fillets on a baking sheet. Surround them with the cherry tomatoes and olives.
3. Drizzle with olive oil and lemon juice, then season with salt and pepper.
4. Bake for 15-20 minutes, or until the fish is flaky and cooked through.
5. Serve hot.

Nutritional Values: Calories: 350 kcal, Protein: 28g, Fiber: 2g, Omega-3 fatty acids: 0.7g

---

Cauliflower and Chickpea Curry

Ingredients:

- 1 head cauliflower, chopped into florets
- 1 can chickpeas, rinsed and drained
- 1 onion, diced
- 2 cloves garlic, minced

- 2 tablespoons curry powder
- 1 can coconut milk
- 1 tablespoon olive oil
- Salt and pepper to taste

Steps:

1. Heat the olive oil in a large pot over medium heat. Add the onion and garlic, cooking until they are soft and fragrant.
2. Stir in the curry powder, then add the cauliflower and chickpeas.
3. Pour in the coconut milk and bring the mixture to a simmer. Cook for 20-25 minutes, or until the cauliflower is tender.
4. Season with salt and pepper, then serve hot.

Nutritional Values: Calories: 400 kcal, Protein: 12g, Fiber: 8g, Omega-3 fatty acids: 0.3g

These dinner recipes are perfect for seniors looking for brain-boosting meals that are easy to prepare and full of flavor. They provide a mix of lean protein, healthy fats, and fiber, all of which contribute to brain health and overall well-being. Enjoy these meals as part of a balanced, brain-healthy diet.

Roasted Eggplant and Tomato Pasta

Ingredients:

- 1 large eggplant, cut into cubes
- 2 cups cherry tomatoes, halved
- 2 cloves garlic, minced
- 2 tablespoons olive oil
- Salt and pepper to taste
- 8 ounces whole grain spaghetti
- Grated Parmesan and fresh basil leaves for serving

Steps:

1. Preheat your oven to 400°F (200°C).
2. Place the eggplant cubes, cherry tomatoes, and garlic on a baking sheet. Drizzle with olive oil, then season with salt and pepper.
3. Roast for 20-25 minutes, or until the vegetables are tender and slightly caramelized.
4. While the vegetables are roasting, cook the spaghetti according to the package instructions.
5. Toss the roasted vegetables with the cooked spaghetti. Top with grated Parmesan and fresh basil leaves before serving.

Nutritional Values: Calories: 400 kcal, Protein: 14g, Fiber: 10g, Omega-3 fatty acids: 0.2g

---

Turkey and Vegetable Stuffed Peppers

Ingredients:

- 4 bell peppers, tops removed and seeds scooped out
- 1 pound lean ground turkey
- 1 zucchini, diced
- 1 onion, diced
- 2 cloves garlic, minced
- 1 cup cooked brown rice
- 1 cup tomato sauce
- 1 tablespoon olive oil
- Salt and pepper to taste

Steps:

1. Preheat your oven to 375°F (190°C).
2. Heat the olive oil in a large skillet over medium heat. Add the ground turkey, zucchini, onion, and garlic, cooking until the turkey is browned and the vegetables are tender.

3. Stir in the cooked brown rice and tomato sauce.
4. Spoon the turkey mixture into the bell peppers, filling them to the top. Place the stuffed bell peppers in a baking dish.
5. Cover with aluminum foil and bake for 30-35 minutes, or until the bell peppers are tender.
6. Serve hot.

Nutritional Values: Calories: 400 kcal, Protein: 30g, Fiber: 6g, Omega-3 fatty acids: 0.3g

Zucchini Noodles with Pesto and Cherry Tomatoes

Ingredients:

- 4 medium zucchinis, spiralized into noodles
- 1 cup cherry tomatoes, halved
- 1/4 cup pesto
- Grated Parmesan for serving

Steps:

1. Cook the zucchini noodles in a large skillet over medium heat for 2-3 minutes, or until they are just tender.
2. Remove from the heat and stir in the pesto until the noodles are well coated.
3. Stir in the cherry tomatoes.
4. Serve hot, topped with grated Parmesan.

Nutritional Values: Calories: 200 kcal, Protein: 6g, Fiber: 4g, Omega-3 fatty acids: 0.2g

These dinner recipes provide a variety of flavors and nutrients to help seniors maintain their brain health. They are also quick and easy to prepare, making them perfect for a hassle-free dinner. Enjoy these nutrient-packed meals for a delicious end to your day!

Garlic Lemon Shrimp with Whole Wheat Orzo

Ingredients:

- 1 pound shrimp, peeled and deveined
- 1 cup whole wheat orzo
- 2 cloves garlic, minced
- Juice of 1 lemon
- 2 tablespoons olive oil
- Salt and pepper to taste
- Fresh parsley for garnish

Steps:

1. Cook the orzo according to the package instructions. Drain and set aside.
2. Heat the olive oil in a large skillet over medium heat. Add the garlic and cook until fragrant, about 1 minute.
3. Add the shrimp and cook until pink, about 2-3 minutes per side.
4. Stir in the lemon juice and season with salt and pepper.
5. Toss the cooked shrimp with the orzo, then garnish with fresh parsley before serving.

Nutritional Values: Calories: 400 kcal, Protein: 30g, Fiber: 5g, Omega-3 fatty acids: 0.4g

Black Bean and Sweet Potato Chili

Ingredients:

- 2 sweet potatoes, peeled and diced
- 1 can black beans, rinsed and drained
- 1 onion, diced
- 2 cloves garlic, minced
- 1 can diced tomatoes
- 1 tablespoon chili powder
- 1 tablespoon olive oil
- Salt and pepper to taste
- Fresh cilantro and Greek yogurt for serving

Steps:

1. Heat the olive oil in a large pot over medium heat. Add the onion and garlic, cooking until they are soft and fragrant.
2. Stir in the sweet potatoes, black beans, diced tomatoes, and chili powder.
3. Cover and simmer for 20-25 minutes, or until the sweet potatoes are tender.
4. Season with salt and pepper, then serve hot with a dollop of Greek yogurt and a sprinkling of fresh cilantro.

Nutritional Values: Calories: 350 kcal, Protein: 12g, Fiber: 10g, Omega-3 fatty acids: 0.3g

Baked Salmon with Lemon Dill Sauce

Ingredients:

- 2 salmon fillets
- Juice of 1 lemon
- 1 tablespoon olive oil
- Salt and pepper to taste

For the Lemon Dill Sauce:

- 1/4 cup Greek yogurt
- 1 tablespoon fresh dill, chopped
- Zest and juice of 1 lemon
- Salt and pepper to taste

Steps:

1. Preheat your oven to 400°F (200°C).
2. Place the salmon fillets on a baking sheet. Drizzle with olive oil and lemon juice, then season with salt and pepper.
3. Bake for 15-20 minutes, or until the fish is flaky and cooked through.
4. While the salmon is baking, prepare the Lemon Dill Sauce by mixing together the Greek yogurt, dill, lemon zest and juice, salt, and pepper.
5. Serve the baked salmon hot with a dollop of the Lemon Dill Sauce.

Nutritional Values: Calories: 400 kcal, Protein: 34g, Fiber: 0g, Omega-3 fatty acids: 1.5g

Enjoy these diverse, nutrient-dense dinner recipes as a delicious way to enhance your brain health. By incorporating a variety of nutrient-rich foods, you're not only taking care of your brain but also your overall well-being. These simple yet flavorful recipes make it easy and enjoyable to maintain a healthy diet.

Chicken and Vegetable Stir Fry

Ingredients:

- 1 pound chicken breast, cut into thin strips
- 2 bell peppers, sliced
- 1 zucchini, sliced
- 1 onion, sliced
- 2 cloves garlic, minced
- 2 tablespoons low-sodium soy sauce
- 1 tablespoon olive oil
- Salt and pepper to taste
- Sesame seeds for garnish

Steps:

1. Heat the olive oil in a large skillet or wok over medium heat.
2. Add the chicken strips and cook until they are no longer pink in the middle, about 5-7 minutes. Remove from the skillet and set aside.
3. In the same skillet, add the bell peppers, zucchini, onion, and garlic. Cook until the vegetables are tender-crisp, about 5 minutes.
4. Return the chicken to the skillet. Add the soy sauce and stir to combine.
5. Season with salt and pepper, then sprinkle with sesame seeds before serving.

Nutritional Values: Calories: 350 kcal, Protein: 30g, Fiber: 5g, Omega-3 fatty acids: 0.3g

Lentil and Vegetable Soup

Ingredients:

- 1 cup green lentils, rinsed
- 2 carrots, diced
- 2 celery stalks, diced
- 1 onion, diced
- 2 cloves garlic, minced
- 4 cups vegetable broth
- 1 can diced tomatoes
- 1 tablespoon olive oil
- Salt and pepper to taste

Steps:

1. Heat the olive oil in a large pot over medium heat. Add the carrots, celery, onion, and garlic, cooking until the vegetables are tender.
2. Stir in the lentils, vegetable broth, and diced tomatoes.
3. Bring the soup to a boil, then reduce the heat and simmer for 30-35 minutes, or until the lentils are tender.
4. Season with salt and pepper, then serve hot.

Nutritional Values: Calories: 300 kcal, Protein: 20g, Fiber: 10g, Omega-3 fatty acids: 0.2g

---

Quinoa Stuffed Bell Peppers

Ingredients:

- 4 bell peppers, tops removed and seeds scooped out
- 1 cup cooked quinoa
- 1 can black beans, rinsed and drained
- 1 cup corn kernels

- 1 cup salsa
- 1 teaspoon cumin
- Salt and pepper to taste
- Fresh cilantro for garnish

Steps:

1. Preheat your oven to 375°F (190°C).
2. In a large bowl, combine the cooked quinoa, black beans, corn, salsa, cumin, salt, and pepper.
3. Spoon the quinoa mixture into the bell peppers, filling them to the top. Place the stuffed bell peppers in a baking dish.
4. Cover with aluminum foil and bake for 30-35 minutes, or until the bell peppers are tender.
5. Serve hot, garnished with fresh cilantro.

Nutritional Values: Calories: 350 kcal, Protein: 15g, Fiber: 9g, Omega-3 fatty acids: 0.3g

These hearty and healthy dinner recipes are packed with brain-boosting nutrients and delicious flavors. They are perfect for seniors who are looking to nourish their brains and bodies while enjoying a variety of tastes and textures. Enjoy these meals as part of your regular diet for a happy and healthy lifestyle.

Greek-Style Baked Cod

Ingredients:

- 4 cod fillets
- 1 lemon, sliced
- 2 tablespoons olive oil
- 1 teaspoon dried oregano
- Salt and pepper to taste
- Fresh parsley for garnish

Steps:

1. Preheat your oven to 400°F (200°C).
2. Arrange the cod fillets on a baking sheet. Drizzle with olive oil and season with oregano, salt, and pepper.
3. Place the lemon slices on top of the cod fillets.
4. Bake for 12-15 minutes, or until the fish is flaky and cooked through.
5. Garnish with fresh parsley before serving.

Nutritional Values: Calories: 230 kcal, Protein: 30g, Fiber: 0g, Omega-3 fatty acids: 1.0g

---

Spinach and Mushroom Frittata

Ingredients:

- 6 eggs
- 2 cups fresh spinach, chopped
- 1 cup mushrooms, sliced
- 1 onion, diced
- 2 cloves garlic, minced
- 1 tablespoon olive oil
- Salt and pepper to taste
- Fresh basil leaves for garnish

Steps:

1. Preheat your oven to 375°F (190°C).
2. Heat the olive oil in a large, oven-safe skillet over medium heat. Add the onions and garlic, cooking until they are soft and fragrant.
3. Stir in the mushrooms and cook until they are tender.
4. Add the spinach and cook until it is wilted.
5. In a large bowl, whisk the eggs and season with salt and pepper. Pour the eggs over the vegetables in the skillet.

6. Transfer the skillet to the oven and bake for 15-20 minutes, or until the frittata is set.
7. Garnish with fresh basil leaves before serving.

Nutritional Values: Calories: 200 kcal, Protein: 12g, Fiber: 2g, Omega-3 fatty acids: 0.2g

Roasted Chicken with Root Vegetables

Ingredients:

- 1 whole chicken
- 2 carrots, chopped
- 2 parsnips, chopped
- 2 potatoes, chopped
- 1 onion, chopped
- 2 tablespoons olive oil
- Salt and pepper to taste
- Fresh rosemary for garnish

Steps:

1. Preheat your oven to 400°F (200°C).
2. Arrange the vegetables in a large roasting pan. Drizzle with one tablespoon of the olive oil and season with salt and pepper.
3. Rub the chicken with the remaining olive oil and season with salt and pepper. Place the chicken on top of the vegetables.
4. Roast for about 1 hour and 30 minutes, or until the chicken is cooked through and the vegetables are tender.
5. Let the chicken rest for a few minutes before carving. Garnish with fresh rosemary before serving.

Nutritional Values: Calories: 400 kcal, Protein: 30g, Fiber: 4g, Omega-3 fatty acids: 0.3g

These dinner recipes combine simple ingredients and cooking techniques to create delicious, nutrient-dense meals. Each recipe is packed with brain-boosting ingredients to help maintain and enhance cognitive health. Enjoy these meals as you journey towards a healthier mind and body!

Tofu Stir-Fry with Broccoli and Bell Peppers

Ingredients:

- 1 block of tofu, cubed
- 2 cups of broccoli florets
- 1 red bell pepper, sliced
- 2 tablespoons low-sodium soy sauce
- 1 tablespoon olive oil
- 2 cloves of garlic, minced
- Salt and pepper to taste
- Sesame seeds for garnish

Steps:

1. Press the tofu to remove excess water, then cut into cubes.
2. Heat the olive oil in a large skillet or wok over medium heat. Add the tofu and cook until golden brown on all sides.
3. Add the broccoli and bell pepper to the skillet, cooking until the vegetables are tender-crisp.
4. Stir in the soy sauce and garlic, then season with salt and pepper.
5. Serve hot, garnished with sesame seeds.

Nutritional Values: Calories: 300 kcal, Protein: 20g, Fiber: 5g, Omega-3 fatty acids: 0.2g

Veggie-Packed Lasagna

Ingredients:

- 8 lasagna noodles, cooked
- 1 zucchini, sliced
- 1 bell pepper, sliced
- 1 onion, sliced
- 2 cups fresh spinach
- 2 cups ricotta cheese
- 1 jar marinara sauce
- 1 cup shredded mozzarella cheese
- 1 tablespoon olive oil
- Salt and pepper to taste

Steps:

1. Preheat your oven to 375°F (190°C).
2. Heat the olive oil in a large skillet over medium heat. Add the zucchini, bell pepper, and onion, cooking until the vegetables are tender.
3. Layer the ingredients in a baking dish in the following order: marinara sauce, lasagna noodles, ricotta cheese, vegetables, spinach, mozzarella cheese. Repeat until all the ingredients are used, ending with a layer of marinara sauce and mozzarella cheese.
4. Cover the baking dish with aluminum foil and bake for 30 minutes. Remove the foil and bake for another 10 minutes, or until the cheese is bubbly and golden brown.
5. Let the lasagna cool for a few minutes before serving.

Nutritional Values: Calories: 400 kcal, Protein: 20g, Fiber: 5g, Omega-3 fatty acids: 0.2g

Garlic Shrimp Pasta

Ingredients:

- 8 ounces whole wheat spaghetti
- 1 pound fresh shrimp, peeled and deveined
- 4 cloves garlic, minced
- 2 tablespoons olive oil
- 1/4 teaspoon red pepper flakes
- Salt and pepper to taste
- Fresh parsley for garnish

Steps:

1. Cook the spaghetti according to the package instructions, then drain and set aside.
2. Heat the olive oil in a large skillet over medium heat. Add the garlic and red pepper flakes, cooking until the garlic is golden and fragrant.
3. Add the shrimp to the skillet and cook until they turn pink, about 2-3 minutes on each side.
4. Stir in the cooked spaghetti and toss until it is well-coated in the garlic and oil. Season with salt and pepper.
5. Serve hot, garnished with fresh parsley.

Nutritional Values: Calories: 400 kcal, Protein: 35g, Fiber: 6g, Omega-3 fatty acids: 0.2g

Lemon Baked Salmon with Asparagus

Ingredients:

- 4 salmon fillets
- 1 bunch asparagus, trimmed
- 2 lemons, sliced
- 2 tablespoons olive oil
- Salt and pepper to taste
- Fresh dill for garnish

Steps:

1. Preheat your oven to 400°F (200°C).
2. Arrange the salmon fillets and asparagus on a baking sheet. Drizzle with olive oil and season with salt and pepper.
3. Place the lemon slices on top of the salmon fillets.
4. Bake for 12-15 minutes, or until the salmon is cooked through and the asparagus is tender.
5. Garnish with fresh dill before serving.

Nutritional Values: Calories: 300 kcal, Protein: 35g, Fiber: 3g, Omega-3 fatty acids: 1.5g

---

Quinoa-Stuffed Bell Peppers

Ingredients:

- 4 bell peppers, tops removed and seeded
- 1 cup quinoa
- 2 cups vegetable broth
- 1 onion, diced
- 2 cloves garlic, minced
- 1 can black beans, drained and rinsed
- 1 can diced tomatoes

- 1 teaspoon cumin
- 1 teaspoon chili powder
- 2 tablespoons olive oil
- Salt and pepper to taste

Steps:

1. Preheat your oven to 375°F (190°C).
2. Cook the quinoa according to the package instructions, using vegetable broth instead of water.
3. Heat the olive oil in a large skillet over medium heat. Add the onion and garlic, cooking until they are soft and fragrant.
4. Stir in the black beans, diced tomatoes, cumin, and chili powder. Cook until the mixture is heated through.
5. Combine the cooked quinoa and bean mixture, then season with salt and pepper.
6. Stuff the bell peppers with the quinoa mixture and arrange them in a baking dish.
7. Bake for 30 minutes, or until the peppers are tender.

Nutritional Values: Calories: 320 kcal, Protein: 14g, Fiber: 10g, Omega-3 fatty acids: 0.3g

Baked Sweet Potato with Chickpea Topping

Ingredients:

- 4 sweet potatoes
- 1 can chickpeas, drained and rinsed
- 1 onion, diced
- 2 cloves garlic, minced
- 1 teaspoon cumin
- 1 teaspoon paprika
- 2 tablespoons olive oil
- Salt and pepper to taste

Steps:

1. Preheat your oven to 400°F (200°C).
2. Prick the sweet potatoes with a fork and place them on a baking sheet. Bake for 45-60 minutes, or until they are soft and cooked through.
3. While the sweet potatoes are baking, heat the olive oil in a large skillet over medium heat. Add the onion and garlic, cooking until they are soft and fragrant.
4. Stir in the chickpeas, cumin, and paprika. Cook until the mixture is heated through, then season with salt and pepper.
5. Slice open the baked sweet potatoes and top them with the chickpea mixture before serving.

Nutritional Values: Calories: 400 kcal, Protein: 12g, Fiber: 10g, Omega-3 fatty acids: 0.2g

---

Roasted Beet and Goat Cheese Salad

Ingredients:

- 4 medium beets, peeled and cut into chunks
- 4 cups mixed salad greens
- 1/2 cup goat cheese, crumbled
- 1/4 cup walnuts, chopped
- 2 tablespoons balsamic vinaigrette
- 2 tablespoons olive oil
- Salt and pepper to taste

Steps:

1. Preheat your oven to 400°F (200°C).
2. Toss the beet chunks with the olive oil, salt, and pepper. Spread them out on a baking sheet and roast for about 30 minutes, or until the beets are tender.

3. Let the beets cool, then arrange them on the salad greens. Top with the crumbled goat cheese and chopped walnuts.
4. Drizzle the balsamic vinaigrette over the salad before serving.

Nutritional Values: Calories: 250 kcal, Protein: 7g, Fiber: 4g, Omega-3 fatty acids: 1g

---

Veggie Fried Brown Rice

Ingredients:

- 2 cups cooked brown rice
- 1 cup mixed frozen vegetables
- 2 eggs, beaten
- 2 tablespoons low-sodium soy sauce
- 2 tablespoons olive oil
- 2 cloves garlic, minced
- Salt and pepper to taste

Steps:

1. Heat 1 tablespoon of the olive oil in a large skillet or wok over medium heat. Add the beaten eggs and scramble until they are cooked through. Remove the eggs from the skillet and set them aside.
2. Heat the remaining olive oil in the skillet. Add the garlic and cook until it's golden and fragrant.
3. Add the frozen vegetables and cook until they are heated through.
4. Stir in the cooked brown rice and scrambled eggs. Pour the soy sauce over the rice mixture and stir until everything is well combined.
5. Season with salt and pepper before serving.

Nutritional Values: Calories: 350 kcal, Protein: 10g, Fiber: 4g, Omega-3 fatty acids: 0.3g

Greek Style Baked Cod

Ingredients:

- 4 cod fillets
- 2 tomatoes, sliced
- 1 onion, sliced
- 1/4 cup Kalamata olives, pitted
- 2 tablespoons olive oil
- 1 tablespoon lemon juice
- 2 cloves garlic, minced
- Salt and pepper to taste
- Fresh oregano for garnish

Steps:

1. Preheat your oven to 400°F (200°C).
2. Arrange the cod fillets in a baking dish. Scatter the tomato slices, onion slices, and olives around the cod.
3. In a small bowl, whisk together the olive oil, lemon juice, and minced garlic. Drizzle this mixture over the cod and vegetables, then season with salt and pepper.
4. Bake for 15-20 minutes, or until the cod is cooked through and flakes easily with a fork.
5. Garnish with fresh oregano before serving.

Nutritional Values: Calories: 250 kcal, Protein: 28g, Fiber: 2g, Omega-3 fatty acids: 0.8g

Roasted Chicken with Sweet Potatoes and Brussels Sprouts

Ingredients:

- 4 chicken thighs
- 2 sweet potatoes, cubed
- 2 cups Brussels sprouts, halved
- 2 tablespoons olive oil
- Salt and pepper to taste
- Fresh thyme for garnish

Steps:

1. Preheat your oven to 400°F (200°C).
2. Arrange the chicken thighs, sweet potato cubes, and Brussels sprouts on a baking sheet. Drizzle with olive oil and season with salt and pepper.
3. Roast for 35-40 minutes, or until the chicken is cooked through and the vegetables are tender.
4. Garnish with fresh thyme before serving.

Nutritional Values: Calories: 400 kcal, Protein: 35g, Fiber: 5g, Omega-3 fatty acids: 0.5g

---

Stuffed Portobello Mushrooms with Quinoa and Spinach

Ingredients:

- 4 large portobello mushrooms, stems removed
- 1 cup cooked quinoa
- 2 cups fresh spinach, chopped
- 1 onion, diced

- 2 cloves garlic, minced
- 2 tablespoons olive oil
- Salt and pepper to taste

Steps:

1. Preheat your oven to 375°F (190°C).
2. Heat the olive oil in a large skillet over medium heat. Add the onion and garlic, cooking until they are soft and fragrant.
3. Stir in the spinach and cook until it is wilted. Combine this mixture with the cooked quinoa, then season with salt and pepper.
4. Arrange the portobello mushrooms on a baking sheet, gill-side up. Spoon the quinoa mixture into the mushroom caps.
5. Bake for 20 minutes, or until the mushrooms are tender.

Nutritional Values: Calories: 200 kcal, Protein: 7g, Fiber: 4g, Omega-3 fatty acids: 0.2g

---

Spicy Lentil Soup

Ingredients:

- 1 cup dried lentils
- 4 cups vegetable broth
- 1 onion, diced
- 2 carrots, diced
- 2 cloves garlic, minced
- 1 teaspoon cumin
- 1/2 teaspoon turmeric
- 1/4 teaspoon cayenne pepper
- 2 tablespoons olive oil
- Salt and pepper to taste

Steps:

1. Heat the olive oil in a large pot over medium heat. Add the onion and carrots, cooking until they are soft.
2. Stir in the garlic, cumin, turmeric, and cayenne pepper. Cook until the garlic is golden and the spices are fragrant.
3. Add the lentils and vegetable broth to the pot. Bring the mixture to a boil, then reduce the heat and simmer for 30 minutes, or until the lentils are tender.
4. Season the soup with salt and pepper before serving.

Nutritional Values: Calories: 200 kcal, Protein: 14g, Fiber: 12g, Omega-3 fatty acids: 0.1g

Desserts

Blueberry Almond Crisp

Ingredients:

- 2 cups fresh blueberries
- 1 cup old-fashioned oats
- 1/2 cup almond meal
- 1/4 cup honey
- 2 tablespoons coconut oil, melted
- 1/2 teaspoon cinnamon
- 1/4 teaspoon salt

Steps:

1. Preheat your oven to 350°F (175°C).
2. Spread the blueberries out in a baking dish.
3. In a separate bowl, combine the oats, almond meal, honey, coconut oil, cinnamon, and salt. Spread this mixture over the blueberries.
4. Bake for 25-30 minutes, or until the topping is golden and the blueberries are bubbly.
5. Serve warm.

Nutritional Values: Calories: 200 kcal, Protein: 4g, Fiber: 4g, Omega-3 fatty acids: 0.3g

Chia Seed Pudding with Fresh Berries

Ingredients:

- 1/4 cup chia seeds
- 1 cup almond milk
- 1 tablespoon honey
- 1 cup fresh mixed berries

Steps:

1. Combine the chia seeds, almond milk, and honey in a bowl. Stir until everything is well mixed.
2. Cover the bowl and place it in the refrigerator for at least 2 hours, or until the chia seeds have absorbed the almond milk and the mixture has thickened to a pudding-like consistency.
3. Top with fresh mixed berries before serving.

Nutritional Values: Calories: 180 kcal, Protein: 5g, Fiber: 10g, Omega-3 fatty acids: 2.4g

---

Dark Chocolate Avocado Mousse

Ingredients:

- 2 ripe avocados
- 1/2 cup unsweetened dark cocoa powder
- 1/4 cup honey
- 2 teaspoons vanilla extract
- A pinch of sea salt
- Fresh berries for garnish

Steps:

1. Scoop out the flesh of the avocados and put it into a food processor or blender.
2. Add the dark cocoa powder, honey, vanilla extract, and sea salt.
3. Blend until the mixture is smooth and creamy.
4. Spoon the mousse into dessert dishes and refrigerate for at least 1 hour before serving.
5. Garnish with fresh berries.

Nutritional Values: Calories: 250 kcal, Protein: 4g, Fiber: 10g, Omega-3 fatty acids: 0.2g

---

Banana and Walnut Bread

Ingredients:

- 2 ripe bananas, mashed
- 1/2 cup walnut halves, chopped
- 1/4 cup honey
- 1/4 cup olive oil
- 2 eggs
- 1 teaspoon vanilla extract
- 1 1/2 cups whole wheat flour
- 1 teaspoon baking soda
- A pinch of sea salt

Steps:

1. Preheat your oven to 350°F (175°C) and grease a loaf pan.
2. In a large bowl, mix together the mashed bananas, chopped walnuts, honey, olive oil, eggs, and vanilla extract.
3. In another bowl, mix together the whole wheat flour, baking soda, and sea salt.
4. Gradually add the dry ingredients into the wet ingredients, stirring just until combined.

5. Pour the batter into the prepared loaf pan and bake for 50-60 minutes, or until a toothpick inserted into the center comes out clean.
6. Allow the bread to cool before slicing.

Nutritional Values: Calories: 250 kcal, Protein: 6g, Fiber: 4g, Omega-3 fatty acids: 1g

Berry and Yogurt Parfait

Ingredients:

- 1 cup fresh mixed berries (like blueberries, strawberries, and raspberries)
- 1 cup Greek yogurt
- 1 tablespoon honey
- 1/4 cup granola
- Mint leaves for garnish

Steps:

1. In a glass or bowl, layer half of the Greek yogurt at the bottom.
2. Add half of the mixed berries on top of the yogurt, then sprinkle half of the granola over the berries.
3. Repeat these layers with the remaining yogurt, berries, and granola.
4. Drizzle honey on top and garnish with mint leaves before serving.

Nutritional Values: Calories: 260 kcal, Protein: 18g, Fiber: 4g, Omega-3 fatty acids: 0.1g

Dark Chocolate Dipped Strawberries

Ingredients:

- 1 pound fresh strawberries
- 8 ounces dark chocolate (70% cocoa or more)
- 1 tablespoon coconut oil

Steps:

1. Rinse the strawberries and pat dry, leaving the stems intact.
2. In a microwave-safe bowl, combine the dark chocolate and coconut oil. Microwave in 30-second intervals, stirring between each, until the chocolate is completely melted.
3. Hold each strawberry by the stem and dip it into the melted chocolate, twisting slightly to let any excess chocolate drip off.
4. Arrange the dipped strawberries on a baking sheet lined with wax paper. Refrigerate for at least 30 minutes, or until the chocolate has hardened.

Nutritional Values: Calories: 100 kcal (per strawberry), Protein: 1g, Fiber: 2g, Omega-3 fatty acids: 0g

---

Cinnamon Apple Baked Oatmeal

Ingredients:

- 2 cups old-fashioned oats
- 1 teaspoon baking powder
- 1 1/2 teaspoons ground cinnamon
- 1/2 teaspoon salt
- 1 cup chopped apple
- 2 cups almond milk
- 1/4 cup honey
- 1 large egg

- 1 teaspoon vanilla extract

Steps:

1. Preheat your oven to 375°F (190°C) and grease a baking dish.
2. In a large bowl, mix together the oats, baking powder, cinnamon, salt, and chopped apple.
3. In a separate bowl, whisk together the almond milk, honey, egg, and vanilla extract.
4. Pour the wet ingredients into the dry ingredients, stirring to combine.
5. Transfer the mixture to the prepared baking dish and bake for 35-40 minutes, or until the top is golden and the oats are set.
6. Serve warm.

Nutritional Values: Calories: 200 kcal, Protein: 5g, Fiber: 4g, Omega-3 fatty acids: 0.3g

---

Healthy Carrot Cake

Ingredients:

- 2 cups grated carrots
- 1 1/2 cups whole wheat flour
- 1/2 cup honey
- 1/2 cup unsweetened applesauce
- 2 eggs
- 1 teaspoon vanilla extract
- 1 teaspoon baking soda
- 1 teaspoon ground cinnamon
- 1/2 teaspoon ground nutmeg
- 1/4 teaspoon salt
- 1/2 cup chopped walnuts

Steps:

1. Preheat your oven to 350°F (175°C) and grease a cake pan.
2. In a large bowl, combine the grated carrots, whole wheat flour, honey, applesauce, eggs, vanilla extract, baking soda, cinnamon, nutmeg, and salt. Mix until well combined.
3. Stir in the chopped walnuts.
4. Pour the batter into the prepared cake pan and smooth the top with a spatula.
5. Bake for 30-35 minutes, or until a toothpick inserted into the center of the cake comes out clean.
6. Allow the cake to cool in the pan before slicing and serving.

Nutritional Values: Calories: 220 kcal, Protein: 5g, Fiber: 3g, Omega-3 fatty acids: 1g

---

Almond Butter and Banana Smoothie

Ingredients:

- 1 ripe banana
- 2 tablespoons almond butter
- 1 cup almond milk
- 1 tablespoon honey
- A handful of ice cubes

Steps:

1. In a blender, combine the banana, almond butter, almond milk, honey, and ice cubes.
2. Blend until smooth and creamy.
3. Pour into a glass and enjoy as a refreshing dessert.

Nutritional Values: Calories: 300 kcal, Protein: 8g, Fiber: 5g, Omega-3 fatty acids: 0.1g

Coconut and Pineapple Sorbet

Ingredients:

- 1 can (20 oz) pineapple chunks in juice
- 1 cup canned coconut milk
- 1/4 cup honey

Steps:

1. Drain the pineapple chunks and save the juice.
2. In a blender, combine the pineapple chunks, coconut milk, and honey. Blend until smooth.
3. Pour the mixture into a loaf pan or similar dish and freeze for 2 hours.
4. Take the pan out of the freezer and stir the mixture, then return to the freezer.
5. Repeat every 30 minutes for the next 2 hours, or until the sorbet is set.
6. Serve in dessert dishes, with a splash of the reserved pineapple juice if desired.

Nutritional Values: Calories: 160 kcal, Protein: 1g, Fiber: 2g, Omega-3 fatty acids: 0g

---

Raspberry and Almond Baked Quinoa

Ingredients:

- 1 cup cooked quinoa
- 1 cup fresh raspberries
- 1/4 cup almond slivers
- 1 cup almond milk
- 2 tablespoons honey
- 1/2 teaspoon almond extract

Steps:

1. Preheat your oven to 350°F (175°C) and lightly grease a baking dish.
2. Spread the cooked quinoa in the bottom of the dish. Sprinkle the raspberries and almond slivers evenly over the top.
3. In a separate bowl, whisk together the almond milk, honey, and almond extract. Pour this mixture over the quinoa, raspberries, and almonds in the dish.
4. Bake for 25-30 minutes, or until the liquid is absorbed and the top is slightly golden.
5. Serve warm or chilled.

Nutritional Values: Calories: 200 kcal, Protein: 6g, Fiber: 5g, Omega-3 fatty acids: 0.2g

Dark Chocolate and Walnut Brownies

Ingredients:

- 1/2 cup unsweetened dark cocoa powder
- 1/4 cup whole wheat flour
- 1/2 cup honey
- 1/4 cup melted coconut oil
- 2 large eggs
- 1 teaspoon vanilla extract
- 1/2 cup chopped walnuts
- A pinch of sea salt

Steps:

1. Preheat your oven to 350°F (175°C) and grease a brownie pan.
2. In a large bowl, mix together the cocoa powder and flour.
3. In a separate bowl, whisk together the honey, coconut oil, eggs, and vanilla extract.

4. Gradually add the wet ingredients to the dry ingredients, stirring until well combined.
5. Fold in the chopped walnuts and salt.
6. Pour the batter into the prepared brownie pan and smooth the top with a spatula.
7. Bake for 15-20 minutes, or until a toothpick inserted into the center of the brownies comes out clean.
8. Allow the brownies to cool in the pan before cutting and serving.

Nutritional Values: Calories: 180 kcal, Protein: 4g, Fiber: 3g, Omega-3 fatty acids: 1g

---

Blueberry and Almond Chia Pudding

Ingredients:

- 1/4 cup chia seeds
- 1 cup almond milk
- 1 tablespoon honey
- 1/2 teaspoon almond extract
- 1/2 cup fresh blueberries
- 2 tablespoons almond slivers

Steps:

1. In a bowl, mix together the chia seeds, almond milk, honey, and almond extract. Let the mixture sit for about 5 minutes, then stir again to prevent the chia seeds from clumping together.
2. Cover the bowl and refrigerate for at least 2 hours, or overnight.
3. Before serving, top the chia pudding with fresh blueberries and almond slivers.

Nutritional Values: Calories: 180 kcal, Protein: 6g, Fiber: 10g, Omega-3 fatty acids: 4g

Avocado and Chocolate Popsicles

Ingredients:

- 1 ripe avocado
- 1/4 cup unsweetened dark cocoa powder
- 1/4 cup honey
- 1 cup almond milk

Steps:

1. Scoop out the flesh of the avocado and put it into a blender.
2. Add the dark cocoa powder, honey, and almond milk to the blender.
3. Blend until the mixture is smooth and creamy.
4. Pour the mixture into popsicle molds and insert sticks.
5. Freeze for at least 4 hours, or until the popsicles are solid.
6. To remove the popsicles from the molds, run the molds under warm water for a few seconds, then gently pull on the sticks.

Nutritional Values: Calories: 150 kcal, Protein: 3g, Fiber: 6g, Omega-3 fatty acids: 0.2g

Greek Yogurt and Berry Ice Cream

Ingredients:

- 2 cups Greek yogurt
- 1/4 cup honey
- 1 cup mixed berries (like blueberries, strawberries, and raspberries)

Steps:

1. In a bowl, combine the Greek yogurt and honey, stirring until well mixed.
2. If you have an ice cream maker, churn the yogurt mixture according to the manufacturer's instructions. About 5 minutes before the ice cream is done churning, add the mixed berries.
3. If you don't have an ice cream maker, pour the yogurt mixture into a loaf pan or similar dish. Stir in the mixed berries, then cover and freeze. Every 30 minutes for the first 2-3 hours, stir the mixture to break up any ice crystals.
4. Serve the ice cream directly from the ice cream maker or the freezer.

Nutritional Values: Calories: 150 kcal, Protein: 10g, Fiber: 1g, Omega-3 fatty acids: 0g

Almond and Apricot Biscotti

Ingredients:

- 1 cup whole almonds
- 1 cup dried apricots, chopped
- 2 cups whole wheat flour
- 1/2 cup honey
- 2 eggs
- 1 teaspoon vanilla extract
- 1 teaspoon baking powder
- 1/4 teaspoon salt

Steps:

1. Preheat your oven to 350°F (175°C) and line a baking sheet with parchment paper.
2. In a large bowl, mix together the whole almonds, chopped apricots, whole wheat flour, honey, eggs, vanilla extract, baking powder, and salt. The dough will be sticky.

3. With wet hands, shape the dough into a log on the prepared baking sheet.
4. Bake for 25-30 minutes, or until the log is lightly golden and firm to the touch.
5. Allow the log to cool for about 10 minutes, then slice it diagonally into 1/2-inch thick slices using a serrated knife.
6. Arrange the slices cut-side down on the baking sheet and bake for another 10-15 minutes, or until the biscotti are crisp and golden.
7. Allow the biscotti to cool completely on a wire rack before serving.

Nutritional Values: Calories: 140 kcal, Protein: 4g, Fiber: 3g, Omega-3 fatty acids: 0.2g

---

Sweet Potato and Walnut Bread

Ingredients:

- 1 cup mashed sweet potato
- 2 cups whole wheat flour
- 1/2 cup honey
- 1/4 cup melted coconut oil
- 2 eggs
- 1 teaspoon vanilla extract
- 1 teaspoon baking soda
- 1 teaspoon ground cinnamon
- 1/2 teaspoon ground nutmeg
- 1/4 teaspoon salt
- 1/2 cup chopped walnuts

Steps:

1. Preheat your oven to 350°F (175°C) and grease a loaf pan.

2. In a large bowl, combine the mashed sweet potato, whole wheat flour, honey, coconut oil, eggs, vanilla extract, baking soda, cinnamon, nutmeg, and salt. Mix until well combined.
3. Stir in the chopped walnuts.
4. Pour the batter into the prepared loaf pan and smooth the top with a spatula.
5. Bake for 45-50 minutes, or until a toothpick inserted into the center of the loaf comes out clean.
6. Allow the loaf to cool in the pan before slicing and serving.

Nutritional Values: Calories: 210 kcal, Protein: 5g, Fiber: 4g, Omega-3 fatty acids: 1g

Peanut Butter Energy Balls

Ingredients:

- 1 cup old-fashioned oats
- 1/2 cup peanut butter
- 1/4 cup honey
- 1/4 cup ground flaxseed
- 1/4 cup mini chocolate chips
- 1/4 cup chopped almonds
- 1 teaspoon vanilla extract
- Pinch of salt

Steps:

1. In a mixing bowl, combine all the ingredients and mix well until fully combined.
2. Cover the bowl and refrigerate the mixture for about 30 minutes to make it easier to handle.
3. Once chilled, roll the mixture into bite-sized balls, about 1 inch in diameter.

4. Place the energy balls on a baking sheet lined with parchment paper.
5. Refrigerate the energy balls for at least 1 hour before serving.
6. Store the energy balls in an airtight container in the refrigerator for up to 2 weeks.
7. Enjoy these nutritious and energizing snacks whenever you need a quick boost!

Nutritional Values: Calories: 120 kcal, Protein: 4g, Fiber: 2g, Calcium: 2%, Iron: 4%

Banana Berry Smoothie

Ingredients:

- 1 ripe banana
- 1 cup mixed berries (strawberries, blueberries, raspberries)
- 1/2 cup Greek yogurt
- 1/2 cup unsweetened almond milk
- 1 tablespoon honey or maple syrup (optional)
- Ice cubes (optional)

Steps:

1. In a blender, combine the ripe banana, mixed berries, Greek yogurt, almond milk, and honey or maple syrup (if desired).
2. Blend until smooth and creamy.
3. If you prefer a colder smoothie, add a handful of ice cubes and blend again until smooth.
4. Pour the smoothie into glasses and serve immediately.
5. It's a refreshing and nutrient-packed treat!

Nutritional Values: Calories: 180 kcal, Protein: 9g, Fiber: 5g, Vitamin C: 25%, Calcium: 15%

Dark Chocolate Avocado Mousse

Ingredients:

- 2 ripe avocados
- 1/4 cup unsweetened cocoa powder
- 1/4 cup honey or maple syrup
- 1 teaspoon vanilla extract
- Pinch of salt
- 1/4 cup almond milk (or any other non-dairy milk)
- Dark chocolate shavings for garnish (optional)

Steps:

1. Scoop out the flesh of the avocados and place them in a blender or food processor.
2. Add the cocoa powder, honey or maple syrup, vanilla extract, salt, and almond milk to the blender.
3. Blend until smooth and creamy, scraping down the sides if necessary.
4. Taste the mixture and adjust the sweetness if needed by adding more honey or maple syrup.
5. Spoon the mousse into serving bowls or glasses.
6. Refrigerate for at least 1 hour to chill and firm up.
7. Garnish with dark chocolate shavings (if desired) before serving.
8. Enjoy this rich and indulgent dessert!

Nutritional Values: Calories: 210 kcal, Protein: 3g, Fiber: 7g, Calcium: 2%, Iron: 6%

Yogurt Parfait with Mixed Berries

Ingredients:

- 1 cup Greek yogurt
- 1/4 cup granola
- 1/4 cup mixed berries (strawberries, blueberries, raspberries)
- 1 tablespoon honey or maple syrup

Steps:

1. In a glass or a bowl, layer 1/4 cup of Greek yogurt at the bottom.
2. Sprinkle 1 tablespoon of granola on top of the yogurt.
3. Add a layer of mixed berries.
4. Repeat the layers with the remaining yogurt, granola, and mixed berries.
5. Drizzle the honey or maple syrup over the top layer.
6. Serve immediately and enjoy this refreshing and protein-packed snack or dessert!

Nutritional Values: Calories: 230 kcal, Protein: 16g, Fiber: 4g, Calcium: 15%, Vitamin C: 10%

Roasted Chickpeas

Ingredients:

- 1 can (15 ounces) chickpeas (garbanzo beans), drained and rinsed
- 1 tablespoon olive oil
- 1 teaspoon ground cumin
- 1/2 teaspoon paprika

- 1/2 teaspoon garlic powder
- Salt to taste

Steps:

1. Preheat your oven to 400°F (200°C) and line a baking sheet with parchment paper.
2. In a bowl, toss the chickpeas with olive oil, cumin, paprika, garlic powder, and salt until evenly coated.
3. Spread the seasoned chickpeas on the baking sheet in a single layer.
4. Roast in the preheated oven for 25-30 minutes, or until golden brown and crispy.
5. Remove from the oven and let the roasted chickpeas cool before serving.
6. Enjoy these crunchy and protein-rich snacks!

Nutritional Values: Calories: 140 kcal, Protein: 6g, Fiber: 5g, Iron: 10%

Strawberry Banana Nice Cream

Ingredients:

- 2 ripe bananas, peeled and frozen
- 1 cup frozen strawberries
- 1/2 cup unsweetened almond milk (or any other non-dairy milk)
- 1 tablespoon honey or maple syrup (optional)

Steps:

1. In a blender or food processor, combine the frozen bananas, frozen strawberries, and almond milk.
2. Blend until smooth and creamy, scraping down the sides as needed.

3. Taste the mixture and add honey or maple syrup if you prefer a sweeter flavor.
4. Blend again until everything is well combined.
5. Transfer the nice cream to a container and freeze for an additional 1-2 hours to firm up.
6. Serve the strawberry banana nice cream in bowls or cones and enjoy this guilt-free frozen treat!

Nutritional Values: Calories: 120 kcal, Protein: 2g, Fiber: 4g, Vitamin C: 60%

Trail Mix Energy Bars

Ingredients:

- 1 cup rolled oats
- 1/2 cup almond butter or peanut butter
- 1/4 cup honey or maple syrup
- 1/4 cup chopped nuts (e.g., almonds, walnuts, cashews)
- 1/4 cup dried fruits (e.g., cranberries, raisins, apricots)
- 1/4 cup mini chocolate chips
- 1/4 teaspoon cinnamon
- Pinch of salt

Steps:

1. In a large bowl, combine the rolled oats, almond butter or peanut butter, honey or maple syrup, chopped nuts, dried fruits, mini chocolate chips, cinnamon, and salt.
2. Mix well until all the ingredients are evenly distributed.
3. Line a baking dish with parchment paper.
4. Transfer the mixture to the baking dish and press it down firmly to create an even layer.
5. Refrigerate the mixture for at least 2 hours, or until it has hardened.

6. Once firm, remove from the refrigerator and cut into bars or squares.
7. Store the trail mix energy bars in an airtight container in the refrigerator for up to 2 weeks.
8. These bars make for a convenient and energizing snack on the go!

Nutritional Values: Calories: 180 kcal, Protein: 5g, Fiber: 3g, Iron: 8%

Dark Chocolate Covered Strawberries

Ingredients:

- 1 cup dark chocolate chips
- 12 fresh strawberries

Steps:

1. Line a baking sheet with parchment paper.
2. In a microwave-safe bowl, melt the dark chocolate chips in 30-second intervals, stirring between each interval, until smooth and melted.
3. Hold each strawberry by the stem and dip it into the melted chocolate, swirling it around to coat the strawberry completely.
4. Lift the coated strawberry and allow any excess chocolate to drip off.
5. Place the chocolate-covered strawberry on the prepared baking sheet.
6. Repeat the process with the remaining strawberries.
7. Once all the strawberries are coated, refrigerate the baking sheet for about 15 minutes, or until the chocolate has set.
8. Serve the dark chocolate covered strawberries as a delectable dessert or sweet treat.

Nutritional Values: Calories: 60 kcal (per strawberry), Protein: 1g, Fiber: 1g, Iron: 4%

Conclusion

Over the course of this book, we've journeyed together through the labyrinth that is dementia and Alzheimer's, from understanding the diseases to navigating their complexities. We've explored how nutrition and dietary habits play a significant role in cognitive health, and we've provided an arsenal of brain-boosting recipes that are not only beneficial but also enjoyable.

Richard Isaacs' manual has empowered you with practical strategies and advice on care. We've explored how to create a dementia-friendly environment, manage stress, and even legally plan for the future. These resources are invaluable, and the learning doesn't stop here.

Living with dementia and Alzheimer's, or caring for someone who does, is a journey of patience, courage, and love. It's our hope that 'Brain-Boosting Bites & Guide' serves as a compass, guiding and supporting you through every step. It is a beacon of hope in challenging times, illuminating the pathway to better mental health and quality of life.

Thank you for letting us be a part of your journey. We believe in the power of knowledge, the strength of community, and, most importantly, the resilience of the human spirit. We encourage you to continue exploring, learning, and, above all, maintaining hope.

Remember, every meal, every strategy, and every small victory brings you one step closer to enhancing cognitive health and transforming the experience of dementia and Alzheimer's disease. Here's to a journey filled with brain-boosting bites and proactive strategies!

Richard Isaacs